GW00731799

JANE Hunter

JANE *Hunter*

Growing a Legacy

TESSA ANDERSON

HarperCollins*Publishers*

National Library of New Zealand Cataloguing-in-Publication Data

Anderson, Tessa, 1960-
Jane Hunter : growing a legacy / Tessa Anderson.
ISBN 978-1-86950-648-3
1. Hunter, Jane. 2. Women vintners—New Zealand—Marlborough
—Biography. 3. Vintners—New Zealand—Marlborough—Biography.
4. Wine and wine making—New Zealand—Marlborough. I. Title.
641.22092—dc 22

First published 2008
HarperCollins*Publishers (New Zealand) Limited*
P.O. Box 1, Shortland Street, Auckland

ISBN 978 1 86950 648 3

Cover design by Matt Stanton, HarperCollins Design Studio
Cover photo by Frank Gasteiger, author photo by Jim Tannock
Typesetting by Springfield West

Printed by Griffin Press, Australia

70gsm Classic used by HarperCollins*Publishers* is a natural, recyclable product
made from wood grown in sustainable forests. The manufacturing processes
conform to the environmental regulations in the country of origin, Finland.

Contents

Foreword

I regard it as a high honour to have been asked to write this foreword to the story of Jane Hunter's immense contribution to the development of New Zealand wine to the internationally respected success status it has achieved to date and will assuredly enhance in the future.

Jane is a talented viticulturist; she is also a beautiful woman, of great intelligence, and has a refined vivacious charm when she allows herself to emerge from a natural reserve verging on shyness. Little wonder that she attracted the attention of expatriate Irishman Ernie Hunter, who was a leading and ebullient light in the then infant Marlborough wine industry. Jane has a number of personal characteristics that stamp her as an outstanding leader: humility, reality, determination, dedication, preparedness to speak out for her beliefs, a willingness to seek and take advice on matters where she doubts her own competence. But above all, loyalty and utmost support to her family, friends, and anyone in whom she has learned to trust.

I know this, because I have the great fortune to count myself as one of those friends.

In a speech she delivered in 1997, when she received an Honorary Doctorate from Massey University, Jane spelt out the philosophy with which she directed the affairs of Hunter's Wines (NZ) Ltd. To me it personifies her many attributes.

'If you study the lives of those throughout the course of history who have made an immortal mark in the world, you will find that, generally, and regardless of their field of endeavour, they were possessed of a basic philosophical motivation. In rugby parlance, we could say they knew the ball they planned to play with, and they kept their eye always on it; they knew how they wanted to play the ball and seldom deviated from their selected tactics.

'But we are more than rugby players. We are the inheritors of a land blessed by Nature as no other, with a unique environment for the production of things to eat and drink, products to sustain life and gladden the heart. More than any lawyer who devises the rules, any accountant who counts the numbers, more than any engineer who designs and makes any one of an increasingly bewildering array of practical inventions, more even than any doctor who heals the sick, we are the people entrusted with the responsibility for leading and guiding what always has been and always will be New Zealand's core activity: the growing of things for people here and beyond our shores to eat and drink.

'In so many food and beverage products already, New Zealand has created an international awareness of differentiation. Our foods and beverages have distinctive taste and composition characteristics which are unique to New Zealand. That distinctiveness has a value in a world of increasing blandness. We must at all times strive to maintain our distinctive New Zealand flavours and composition, not only as a matter of pride, but also as a matter of the competitive edge which creates economic advantage.

'The entry of Britain into the Common Market all those years ago gave us our most salutary lesson in primary production: that we will get paid for our products only what consumers of the world are prepared to pay. Affordability is achieved by a combination of production efficiency, realistic planning, and creative marketing. Affordability doesn't mean that we have to compete at the lowest level; what it does mean is that we have to demonstrate value for money in the highest niches of the market we can attain, niches which are available for products which are distinctive and of high quality.

'But above all, we must dedicate ourselves to quality; consistent, recognisable, internationally acknowledged quality, even if, in contrast to the so-called free market ideology of the day, that means that we have to legislate minimum quality standards to protect the reputation of New Zealand from damage by occasional irresponsible cowboys whose only motivation is a fast buck.'

Jane's story is one that mirrors the emergence of the Marlborough wine industry. In a few short years she had gone from being an unknown individual to being feted as one of the great women in wine. She has overcome adversity and personal tragedy to forge a career and business that is admired the world over. But throughout it all, she has retained the humility, honesty and determination that were hallmark characteristics that first brought her to the attention of Ernie back in 1983. Her story is one that fully deserves telling.

Terry Dunleavy, MBE, JP, FWINZ

Acknowledgements

Nothing can be achieved without the contribution of many people and my story is no exception. In the telling I have no doubt omitted the names of many people who in their own way have helped me over the years. That in no way belittles the contribution they made, but inevitably only a finite number of events and people can be mentioned. There are so many individuals I need to thank, for without them I wouldn't be the person I am today:

The countless people who have supported promotions, wine dinners and wine-tastings in so many countries around the world and whose support for our brand and us has been truly amazing, humbling at times.

The team at Hunter's, who are the backbone of the company and are diligent, enthusiastic and most of all fun. You may not think that I noticed all your hard work but I did and recognised that I was only free to travel promoting the wines because you got on and did what you had to do.

My friends and family have been my strength. They were able to recognise when I needed support and time out and organised me accordingly!

This book is dedicated to my family — my father Brian, my mother Lynne, my stepfather Brian, my sister Libby and her husband Mac, my nephews James and Edward, my sister Ashley and her husband Ian and my partner Graeme.

To my late husband Ernie, and my faithful companions Paddy, Commodore, Pinot, Sooty, Sweep and Pushie Kat.

'You are the wind beneath my wings.'

Jane Hunter OBE

Prologue

It was Commodore who first heard the knock. Dragging his entire 95 kg off the couch where he was sleeping, he lumbered to the front door. It had been the sound of tyres on the gravel that had woken him. That combined with the noise of the V8 engine which signalled his master was home again after another two-week absence. The St Bernard plodded out prepared to give a rapturous welcome home, only to be confounded by the knock. Surely his master hadn't forgotten his keys?

The same sense of confusion was clouding Jane's mind, wondering who on earth would come visiting at midnight. It wasn't unusual for Ernie to have visitors as late as this but he wasn't home. Confusion was replaced by dread when she opened the door to face two policemen. She didn't need to ask; the answer was written on the men's faces. Before a word had been spoken Jane knew that Ernie, her husband of three years, wasn't coming home. In that one moment the axis of her world changed irrevocably.

Ernie, the gregarious larger-than-life Irishman whom she had married in 1984, had died in a head-on crash on the Christchurch motorway.

It was only a few days since she had last seen him, kissing him goodbye at Melbourne International Airport. The couple had been on one of their rare holidays together catching up with Jane's family and doing what Ernie did best, selling wine. While Jane had come home to her job at Montana in Blenheim, Ernie saw an opportunity to sell wine in Tasmania. Never one to give up such a chance, he stayed on a few extra days before flying home to Christchurch. Instead of heading back to Blenheim immediately he stayed in the Garden City for a few days to conduct some business. On Monday night he decided to head for home despite protests from friends who believed he wasn't in a state to drive the four hours. He should have stayed put and driven up the next day, but in typical Ernie fashion he was in a rush. His impatience cost him his life.

It was an explosive end to an explosive life. Ernie was only thirty-eight years old, Jane thirty-three.

His death, while a shock to all who knew him, was in many ways not unexpected. He lived life on the edge, always pushing the boundaries. When Jane rang his father Bill, in Belfast, he told her he had been expecting such a call. Ernie had had so many near misses as he lived life at a million miles an hour, it was to be expected he would never live to see old bones. 'Ernie was always a daredevil and he wasn't the best of drivers. It's not something you think about but I guess if I had thought about it, something was bound to happen,' Jane says.

From the moment she opened the door to face two stoic policemen, she existed in a miasma. People came and went, the phone rang continually, family overseas desperately tried to get flights to New Zealand and flowers arrived by the hundreds. So much so that Blenheim's florists couldn't fill all the orders — they literally ran out of stock. Workmates, associates, wine industry personnel and friends tried desperately to deflect some of the burden of trying to arrange a funeral that would fit in with family arrivals. It was all too much for Jane, a somewhat timid, shy and quietly spoken woman. 'It's all a bit of a blur really. People came from everywhere, people that I wouldn't have really called my friends but they were friends of Ernie's. They made sure I wasn't alone.'

Jane had only been in New Zealand for a few years. All her immediate family lived overseas. Her mother and stepfather lived in Italy, her father, uncles and sisters were all in Australia and then there was Ernie's family — based in Belfast, Ireland. The funeral had to wait for them all to arrive. Finally, a week after his death, the world got to say goodbye to Ernest Christopher Hunter.

Even that is a blur to Jane. She remembers they sang 'How Great Thou Art', and the 23rd Psalm was read. Terry Dunleavy, the CEO of the Wine Institute of New Zealand, gave the eulogy, and hundreds attended. Following his wishes, Jane arranged for Ernie to be cremated. 'He had said to me he never wanted to be buried. He was such a free spirit, I didn't want to do that to him either.'

An Irish wake was inevitable given Ernie's propensity for a drink or two. For some of his friends it lasted two days. For Jane it was enough after a few hours. Especially when she was confronted by an employee of the Public Trust within hours of the funeral, who said he had to arrange a meeting to sort out the ownership of Hunter's. 'I couldn't take any more. I just wanted to get out of there.'

She left, but a large number of Ernie's friends stayed on at Hunter's Restaurant, helping themselves to the wines that had made him a household name. Stories and tales of his escapades and achievements flowed almost as freely as the wine. Ernie may have died — but there were plenty who would never forget his sense of humour, loyalty, sheer gall, fiery temper, generosity, enthusiasm and determination. Wine writers throughout the country were quick to extol his achievements. Described as New Zealand's unofficial wine ambassador, he had developed a wine company that had made the world sit up and take notice and in the process launched Marlborough as a quality wine-producing region. Montana's chief executive Bryan Mogridge described Ernie as a 'rampant attack on the world'.

Without him, could Hunter's survive?

Chapter 1

Budburst

*The beginning of the vine's cycle, when
the first shoots appear on the canes*

When Ernie Hunter arrived in New Zealand in 1972, Marlborough had not even been considered as a potential wine-growing region. With smooth plains, braided by rivers and bounded by naturally imposing hills that create an ever-changing palette of colours, Marlborough's landscape at the time was dotted with sheep and punctuated by crops.

Within twelve months, though, this little forgotten rural corner of New Zealand would be on its way to becoming the talk of the wine industry.

For the Irishman who had left a country racked by political and religious strife, the emergence of a new wine region was probably the last thing on his mind. Little did he know that the machinations of Montana, New Zealand's largest wine company, would eventually change his life both professionally and personally. The choice of Marlborough as a potential wine region was initially investigated by Montana with cloak-and-dagger-style secrecy. The company was keen to expand its holdings in New Zealand but land prices in the known wine regions of the North Island were considered exorbitant. The Board of Directors began looking outside Gisborne and Hawke's Bay for suitable land that would be cost effective. The investigation turned up the possibility of Marlborough, a small rural land base better known for its high sunshine hours than anything else. Sunshine, combined with a variety of soil types ranging from silty alluvial loams over gravelly sub soils through to clay and compacted silts, promised exciting new grape-growing possibilities. The decision was made to buy as much suitable land as possible without anyone knowing they were the interested party. Basically they wanted to ensure there wasn't a blow-out in land prices. To achieve that goal they began to make enquiries under the auspices of a dummy company, Cloudy Bay Developments. Their first point of contact was the Blenheim real estate firm Pyne Gould Guinness. The job of finding the land was given to John Marris, a young stock agent keen on getting into real estate. He was asked if he could locate up to 1200 hectares of land within the next twenty-four hours. John did better than that; he rang his farming clients and within the time frame came up with a potential 2900 hectares. After visiting the region, Montana settled on 1173 hectares, paying out a total of $1,345,425.00 — an average of $1146.00 a hectare. Those farmers who did sell were extremely happy with the deal, especially given the average price for a hectare of farmland in Marlborough at that time was around $250.00.

It was the beginning of the Marlborough wine industry.

As Montana was making its moves into the sleepy little hamlet of Marlborough, Ernie was settling into his new life in Wellington. The twenty-three-year-old was already establishing himself as a man once met, never forgotten. Oozing personality, Ernie had the appearance of a man who didn't really care about his looks. With tousled grey hair, beguiling smile, and eyes that were always in laugh mode, he exuded vigour. He was the embodiment of Irish personality both good and bad, and it's fair to say he had the type of personality that spawns legends. But there was another side to Ernie. He had the cunning of a fox according to many who did business with him. And his fiery temper was renowned.

'Boy could he blow,' says Bill Walsh, the first grower to supply Ernie with grapes. Describing Ernie as being like a son to him, Bill says his close relationship didn't ensure his immunity from temperamental blasts. 'We had some real beaut arguments I can tell you. But once he got it off his chest he was back to his charming self. And boy could he charm. He had more charm in his little finger than most people have in their entire bodies.'

There were few people who knew Ernie who didn't suffer from his temper at some stage or other. According to Jane he was always falling out with people.

But that made him even more interesting, says his lawyer David Dew, who despite his professional position was also not saved from Ernie's temper. 'With Ernie, when things were going smoothly he didn't like it. If there wasn't something happening, a bit of conflict, he would get upset. But then again he would always apologise and if we had had a row he would arrive with a bottle of wine the next day.'

The Irish personality went far beyond the charm and lilting accent. Ernie was also the classic storyteller. Just how much of what he told you was the truth, however, is debatable. But that again was part of his charm. Well-known music entrepreneur and close friend Stewart MacPherson says you took everything he told you with a pinch of salt. 'Sometimes it was a shovelful of salt. He would definitely embellish a story — to make it fit.'

For all that, though, Ernie was one of the most entertaining people you could come across. David Dew says law practice was never the same after Ernie died. 'He would probably have been the most entertaining client you could ever have. But at the same time he was the most trying. He would ring you up at three in the morning with a bright idea and want you to act on it. Then he would arrive the next morning with bottles of French Champagne to apologise for ringing so late. He was entertaining and interesting and I guess you don't come across many people like that in your lifetime.'

Born in Ulster in 1949, Ernie was the second of three children. His father was a Protestant policeman, his stepmother a Catholic teacher. He told friends there had been occasions when parties from both sides of the fence threatened to blow the family home up. But given Ernie's propensity to exaggeration it's unsure whether there is any truth in that.

Maybe it isn't surprising that Ernie ended up on this side of the world, given how difficult times were in Ireland in the early 1970s. You were a marked man no matter which side of the fence you sat on. Managing to stay friendly with both Catholics and Protestants, he kept out of the secular fighting. Honing what were to become his trademark entrepreneurial skills, he took on odd jobs as a youngster and by the time he was sixteen he had his own bank account. That may not seem like much but in Ireland it was a huge deal, as banks were not supposed to open accounts for minors. Maybe more of the Hunter blarney had paved the way.

Musically inclined (though not in terms of playing), Ernie owned a music store, which in turn was the front for him running dances, becoming a sound engineer and touring bands. He knew the price of any instrument you cared to ask for, even if he could never play a single note on any of them. While he has been described as generous to a fault, he wasn't a man to try to cheat, as clients were quick to discover. Despite curfews, Ernie would think nothing of using the night hours to repossess items if he had to.

It was on one such night that he came across two young boys standing in the street, hurling abuse at each other and exchanging punches. Though barely old enough to talk, the boys had learned the permeating hatred towards opposite religions and were vocalising that in true Irish style. It disgusted Ernie and he would later say it summed up what Ireland had become. It was time to get out.

His Uncle Ernie, who had been in the merchant navy, had passed on tales of this magic land at the bottom of the earth. A land where anything was possible, where the people were friendly and the opportunities endless. Ernie's older brother Ian had already been swept up with the magic of his uncle's tales and was currently living in New Zealand. Ernie was determined to join him. 'He always said if he had stayed in Ireland, he would have had to take one side or the other, that was his personality,' Jane says. 'So he decided it was time to get out.'

Ernie set about selling his prized possessions, which included three cars, and making his travel plans to leave his homeland. While he would return three times in the next fifteen years, Ernie would never stay for more than a week. He said goodbye to his old life and began preparing to welcome in his new one in New Zealand's capital, Wellington. Initially he got into the restaurant trade and later had what Stewart MacPherson describes as a 'very dodgy disco on Oriental Parade'. But Wellington wasn't what Ernie had expected. He stayed put for only twelve months, before the lure of the South called him. He moved to Christchurch, where his first foray into business was to establish a fruit and vegetable market. There is little opportunity for an entrepreneurial, party-loving Irishman in the fruit and veggie market, so it comes as no surprise that Ernie quickly began looking further afield. And for someone of his nature, the liquor industry was just the thing. With two fellow Irish expatriates and a pooling of resources, Ernie took over the ownership of Warner's Imperial Hotel and Bottle Store.

Together the three men began to revolutionise the liquor trade, which up until this time had been very much a closed shop. Prices were set and adhered to by all outlets, something that was anathema to Ernie. He began discounting spirits and, in particular, beer. Other outlets were forced to do the same, to ensure they kept their clientele. The discounting continued until it reached almost ludicrously low levels. In the end, discounted prices weren't enough to attract new clients so Ernie had to come up with new marketing ideas. Promotions such as placing a grand piano in the bar, via the roof (it got far more publicity than bringing it through the doors), helped, but it was only a one off. He needed something even more novel, so he came up with the idea of giving away a free chicken with every crate of beer bought. The only problem was that Ernie forgot to explain the chickens weren't frozen. In fact, they weren't even dead. It wasn't long before an official tapped him on the shoulder and explained to the charismatic Irishman that maybe it wasn't such a good look for customers to be leaving Warner's Imperial Bottle Store lugging a crate of beer under one arm and a live chicken under the other.

His entrepreneurial skills weren't limited to the discounting of alcohol. Ernie also claimed to have established New Zealand's first singles bar as well as Canterbury's first wine bar. It was at this time he became acquainted with Bill Turner, a man almost double Ernie's age. Bill owned a small lifestyle block on the outskirts of Christchurch, ironically in a suburb called Belfast. An entrepreneur in his own right, he was growing fruit, flowers and vegetables, with a stall servicing traffic on the main highway. He was also producing cider and apple wines, which were in stock at Warner's Bottle Store. By 1976 he had established a trial five-hectare block of grapes — the second commercial vineyard in Christchurch.

Chatting about the potential, Bill and Ernie saw the

need to extend the range of wines and ciders Bill was currently producing. By this stage Marlborough's first grapes had come on stream and the reaction to the ensuing wines had been positive. Ernie decided if Bill could grow grapes in Canterbury, he would look at investing in Marlborough. Then maybe they could blend the two regions together using Bill's cider factory as a winery. On one of his many visits to Marlborough he went ahead and purchased a substantial 26-hectare block of land in the heart of Rapaura. In 1979 this area was renowned for its barley and lucerne. These days it is known as the Golden Mile of the Marlborough wine industry. The land was expensive at $3000 a hectare, almost double the price of other rural land being sold at the time. In typical Ernie fashion, he didn't have the money to pay for the purchase, so he arranged a delayed settlement. The first payment of $50,000 was due in 1982, the remainder was delayed until 1985. In the meantime, he had to pay rent on the property and homestead that was included with the land. With the luck of the Irish, some could say, land prices rose substantially in the following years and by the time he came to pay for his block it had become somewhat of a bargain.

Still based in Christchurch, Ernie commuted to Blenheim to oversee the planting of (Rhine) Riesling, Gewürztraminer, Müller Thurgau, Cabernet Sauvignon and later Sauvignon Blanc. Despite his investment in the region, he had no initial intention of basing himself in Marlborough. Instead, he intended trucking his fruit to Christchurch and, along with Bill Turner, creating wines to rock the New Zealand market. By the end of 1981, the vineyard was planted and Ernie was starting to revel in his role as a landowner. He decided his quaint Marlborough homestead was the perfect spot for a New Year's Eve party. Among the many guests were two young Germans who had been holidaying in New Zealand. Almuth Lorenz and Thomas Reckart were winemakers and had been brought to the party by Steve Carter, Penfolds New Zealand's South Island Viticultural Manager. Just prior to midnight, before all the kissing and Auld Lang Synes started, Almuth and Thomas singled Ernie out to thank him for the evening. Inevitably the conversation turned to winemaking — something that was on Ernie's mind at the time. Almuth apparently told him she was a winemaker and challenged him to make some wine. Full of bluster, especially after hours of drinking, Ernie agreed to her suggestion. She must have made quite an impression because despite the party and the inevitable sore head the next morning, he didn't forget their conversation. Neither did the young German. Three-and-a-half months later she was ensconced in Bill Turner's old cider factory in Belfast, desperately trying to make the most of the antiquated equipment Ernie had procured to make wine. Perhaps antiquated is too kind a word. After vintage, Ernie described the equipment as 'bloody prehistoric'. Everything was either former cider-making gear or borrowed pieces from a friend's brewery.

Grapes were brought in from Marlborough and blended with those from Bill Turner's Lochbuie property. Arriving in an ale tanker in the middle of the night, they were juiced in an old apple screwpress before settling in former beer tanks. When it came time to bottle the wine there was no sophisticated mechanisation. Almuth, Ernie and Bill did it all by hand prior to placing the hastily created Hunter's Wine labels on the bottles, again by hand.

It was a vintage of passion and that must have shown in the wines, because from that first vintage Hunter's won six medals at the National Wine Show, three silver and three bronze. The 1982 Müller Thurgau Dry was just a fraction off being awarded gold. If Ernie ever needed confirmation he was doing the right thing, the wine awards were it. He was completely and totally hooked. The man of a 'million dreams' had big plans. 'He said to Almuth, as the legend goes, that if you want to come back and make wine in New Zealand, then I will build you a winery,' Jane says.

Known for his ability to exaggerate, it's to Almuth's credit that she did actually return in early 1983. And true to his word, Ernie had built her a winery. But not without encountering rural prejudices and jealousy. In October 1982, with his wine awards under his belt, Ernie applied to the Waimairi District Council (which administered the area north of Christchurch) to build a new winery. The site was 97A Englefield Road, a rural-based area on the outskirts of the Belfast suburb. These days the area is renowned for its expensive homes and beautiful gardens. Back then, though, it seemed the perfect spot for a winery, well away from the hustle and bustle of urban life. Ernie's aim was to produce 12,500 cases annually from the winery, and he planned to sell his liquor industry interests in Christchurch to fund the building.

There were numerous objections and the Council didn't appear enthusiastic about the possibility of a winery within its boundaries. What's more, the Canterbury wine industry wasn't too keen either. The fact that Ernie had blended Marlborough and Canterbury grapes was just too much for some of them to deal with. Choking on their Rieslings, they complained that he was 'destroying the purity of Canterbury's name as a top wine region' by using Marlborough grapes. It all got too difficult. While Ernie wanted to capitalise on the 1982 medals, he needed a winery that was less prehistoric than the former cider factory and he needed it in time for the upcoming harvest. There seemed to be no alternative — he would have to move. If he wasn't allowed to bring Marlborough grapes to Canterbury, then he would build his winery at the source.

Ever aware of his promise to Almuth, Ernie just

managed to get the building complete before she arrived back in the country in time for the 1983 vintage. She was hoping for something more reliable than the previous year but she was to be disappointed. Okay, there weren't the antiquated screwpresses or the necessity to hand bottle, but once again the equipment was old, borrowed and made to fit. If 1982 had been a nightmare, 1983 was only marginally better. The wines, though, weren't.

After tasting success the year before, Ernie had to face reality — the wine industry does not reward complacency. It wasn't all a disaster: Hunter's did get some medals, but they were all bronzes. There were to be no golds, and no silvers. The lack of golds wasn't the only issue Ernie faced. He also had to cope with spiralling interest rates, as Robert Muldoon's National Government desperately tried to get inflation under control. Ernie may well have borrowed money from the bank at 7 per cent interest, but by the end of 1983 that interest was heading towards 20 per cent. By 1984 it would eventually hit 29 per cent. It was a crippling time for any new business. Even more so for Ernie, who had borrowed the money and now had to somehow sell some wine to achieve an income.

Chapter 2

*A winemaking process that filters out
particle matter or yeast from wine*

While Ernie was settling himself into New Zealand life, across the Tasman Jane was zigzagging her way through myriad career choices.

An attractive woman, Jane is diminutive in height and somewhat retiring in demeanour. Her steely determination is not obvious to the casual acquaintance, although there are times when her startling blue eyes move from laughing to penetrating, reminding you there is a steel-trap mind behind the sweet facade.

Home for her was Cobdogla, a tiny township in the heart of the Riverland wine-growing region on the border of South Australia and Victoria. Prior to the Second World War, the area was renowned for the production of dried fruits: raisins, sultanas and blackcurrants. The devastation wreaked upon Europe during the conflict was the impetus for many immigrants to seek new beginnings in places such as Australia. Inevitably, many of those immigrants sought to emulate their European lifestyle, creating a decade of change that saw the Riverland dried-fruit industry begin morphing into what is now a thriving wine industry.

Jane's father, Brian Arnold, is a second-generation man of the land, although his forebears had one foot firmly on the land with the other planted smack in the middle of the Murray River. The Arnold family's ties to South Australia began way back in the 1800s, when Brian's grandfather arrived from Sweden. His move to the Antipodes followed his blacklisting at home, for having started a strike. On his travels around the new country, he journeyed alongside the Murray and recognised the need for some form of boat transport. Within a matter of months he established a fleet of paddle boats on the stretch of water that was the lifeblood of the region. As was often the way in those times, sons followed in their fathers' footsteps and Brian's own father gained his captain's ticket and plied the river also. By the time Brian left school during the war, the glory days of the paddle boat had been overtaken by other forms of transport, and he turned his hand back to the land and dried-fruit industry that was the economic backbone of the region. 'Originally I grew dried fruit, but found that every now and again we would have a bad season and the fruit wouldn't be good enough to dry,' he says. 'So the first distillery was built to turn the grape juice into spirit alcohol and the area became known for its production of brandy.'

The spirit alcohol was also utilised to fortify wines, which in turn were shipped to European countries. 'In the early days with slow ships, we were able to transport all the wines without having to worry about deterioration.'

It wasn't until well into the 1950s that table wine began emerging in the Riverland. Brian, like many of his neighbours, accepted the need for change and began replanting his dried-fruit orchard with vines for wine, although he never gave up on the dried-fruit production altogether.

With hostile climatic conditions that saw the mercury climb well into the 40s during summer and months go by without rain, the Riverland was ideal for both red and white varieties. The Arnold property was home to both, as Brian never trusted the public's palate. 'It's very fickle. One year they would want white wine, the next red.'

It was into this dry, dusty, unforgiving landscape, sprouting vines and the inevitable eucalypts, that Jane was born — two months early. She was the second of three girls spread over six-and-a-half years. Libby, the eldest, remembers Jane as a sickly child who caught every bug and infection doing the rounds. 'She used to receive a lot of attention because she had a lot of medical problems. Not serious ones, just the sort that knocked her around.'

Growing up on the family vineyard she was surrounded by extended family, with three uncles and a fair number of cousins living close by. Her younger sister, Ashley, says it was a pretty idyllic lifestyle. 'We had a lake nearby and an open irrigation channel that had willow trees to hold the banks together. When we were in primary school we used to come home and go swimming in the channel. An uncle next door had a tennis court and we often used to go over there to play. The climate lent itself to lots of outdoor activities. We would go camping, water skiing and sailing.'

All three girls were roped in to help on the vineyard and as soon as they were tall enough for their feet to reach the pedals of the tractor they were driving between the rows while the many Greek and Italian immigrants helped pick the grapes. Some of the workers would come back year after year, helping to instil in Jane a love of European food and language. There was a certain romanticism about these times, which she now associates with the smell of tomatoes, basil and garlic. But, she is quick to add, that is where the romanticism of the industry begins and ends for her. The rest of the year was simply back-breaking work, with the family's entire livelihood wrapped up in a crop that relied heavily on Mother Nature. That strong sense of reality about the wine industry has stood her in good stead in the many years since childhood. It is the reason she never considered viticulture as a suitable career choice. 'I only ever saw it as hard work.'

Shy and reserved, Jane was not one to create a lasting memory as a child. Brian says she was the sort of child that 'would be hiding behind her mother's dress'. Her mother Lynne Chatterton describes her as 'somewhat serious with a sense of humour. She was always determined about her likes and dislikes.' There was no whirlwind of activity surrounding her. She was more content sailing or water-skiing on the nearby lake, or reading, tucked up in a forgotten corner of the vineyard. Even her natural bent in the field of science befits a child with a quiet, thoughtful personality. With her older and younger sisters both very outgoing, Jane was quite happy to foster her own self-sufficiency. While her junior years were spent at the local Cobdogla primary school with eighty other pupils, Jane spent her teenage years boarding in Adelaide at St Peter's Girls School. Despite it being an all-girls' school governed by an order of Anglican nuns, she proudly says she didn't come out with knowledge in cooking, sewing or painting. Instead she left high school with the self-belief she could do anything she wanted, and the confidence to achieve that. Her parents, who divorced when Jane was at secondary school, fostered a thirst for higher education, something Jane is ever grateful for. 'My mother was not a conventional role model for me and my two sisters. She returned to school and university and in fact graduated on the same day that I did. She pursued a career in journalism against many odds, as we lived in a very small rural community. I was free of all family pressure to toe the usual feminine role and in fact my father insisted that his three daughters get a tertiary education so that we would be able to look after ourselves.'

Jane had no yearning to go to university; in fact if her father hadn't been adamant that she get a degree, she would have been more than happy to be driving the tractor on the family vineyard. Faced with the prospect of going to Adelaide to study, Jane was racked with uncertainty over which path to follow. With her leaning towards science, becoming a doctor was an option. But a serious accident involving her cousin threw up all the horrors of medicine and made Jane re-evaluate. The accident did highlight another potential career though — physiotherapy. Within four months of undertaking her science degree towards physio, she says boredom overtook her. 'I realised I didn't have the patience for it.'

With just a subtle shift in focus, she moved into agricultural science, envisaging herself working with farm animals. As a career choice it was a good one for someone who had a natural love of animals and a desire to work on the land. With the degree not confined to the lecture room, Jane and her classmates had to take their theoretical skills and put them to the test on a variety of rural properties in both Australia and New Zealand. It was during one of these practical sessions that Jane decided she had once again made a huge mistake. 'I went to work on a farm way over on the west coast of South Australia. It was about fifty degrees and we were out in the middle of nowhere, with great big cattle beasts stomping around. I thought there has to be something better than this.'

Now two years into her degree, she decided maybe it was better the devil you know than the one you don't. She elected to transfer over to the viticulture course. Not that she ever intended having anything to do with the wine industry. Instead, Jane saw the viticulture course as giving her the opportunity to follow in her mother's footsteps, as a rural journalist for the Australian Broadcasting Commission (ABC). It was standard practice for the ABC to take on a number of agricultural science graduates each year . . . with the exception of 1975, the year Jane graduated. Her dreams of utilising her knowledge in agriculture, viticulture and business management were dashed. Her initial reaction was to head back to Cobdogla and help Brian on his twenty-hectare vineyard. 'She came home and handed me her gown and said, I've come home. I said, if you've come home then I'm going. The vineyard just isn't big enough for two of us, especially for someone with your skills,' Brian remembers.

He says it was the only serious argument he and Jane ever had.

Many of her fellow agricultural science graduates had decided to go back to university and expand their degree. Jane had no desire for that. Instead, she resolved to utilise the skills she had and undertook a teaching diploma. Her decision proved to be the right one, and while she was studying she was also helping the Department of Further Education, Adelaide, to develop a correspondence course in viticulture and business management. The course was subsidised by primary producer boards, wineries and education authorities. Jane was responsible for writing the core material, which in turn was used by Community Colleges throughout the state as the basis for contract teaching. Not only was she responsible for devising the material, she was also responsible for conveying it in a classroom situation. One day a week she taught horticulture and business management to high-security prisoners at Adelaide Prison. The prisoners were growing produce for the School of Food and Catering in Adelaide, and required the business and horticultural skills to ensure success. In reference to her past career choices, Jane says the prisoners were 'easier to control than cattle beasts'.

Eyeing the success of the correspondence programme, New Zealand education authorities were keen to establish a similar venture. They lured Jane across the Tasman with the promise of a position in Wellington that would allow her to develop a comparable programme.

As Jane admits to becoming bored easily, the

opportunity to change countries and lifestyle, while continuing to follow her career path, was a great attraction for her. In mid-1980 she packed up her belongings, including her beloved cat Sooty, and left Australia, only to discover the New Zealand education system was not what she expected. Adelaide's correspondence course systems were not reciprocated in Wellington, which meant Jane spent a frustrating six months going absolutely nowhere. In terms of viticulture, there wasn't the depth within the New Zealand industry to require such a course. 'Within six months nothing had eventuated and I realised it just wasn't going to work.'

Having made the move away from Australia though, Jane wasn't about to pack up and shift home. Once again she began evaluating her choices and when a small shop in Waikanae, north of Wellington, came on the market, she decided to lease it to establish a small cafe. It was rather a game move given she had had nothing to do with the hospitality industry up until then.

Brian came over and helped with the renovations and within weeks of buying the property, she opened the doors to Tootlebury's. Confessing to being no cook, Jane set about revolutionising the small seaside town. She offered quiche, pâté, plunger coffee and what was to become her famous lemon meringue pie. Everything was produced in the open kitchen, which in itself was innovative for early 1980s New Zealand. Seating only thirty people, the cafe was small in terms of potential clientele. But it soon became an iconic venue for Wellingtonians who had weekend homes along the rugged coastline. 'Back then, Saturday was a big day, because Wellington shops would close and shops up the coast, north of the city, were open. We would get hordes of people from the city coming up for the day or weekend.'

Jane soon realised there was a need for evening meals as well as daytime coffee and quiche. She began offering takeaway dinners, which were quickly snapped up by people travelling up the coast late on a Friday night. When that proved a success, she began organising theme dinners, producing French, Italian, or Indian fare. It was an Indian night that nearly lost her the cafe. Having prepared as much of the meal as she could, she headed home to have a rest, only to be dragged back within an hour by the fire brigade. She had forgotten to turn off one of the pots and smoke was billowing out of the cracks under the door. Breaking their way in, the brigade managed to douse the smouldering fire before any major damage was incurred. 'It was a case of the Indian being hotter than I had planned.'

Coming so close to a disaster alerted Jane to the fact she needed a break. A close friend from university was working in America and had been cajoling her to visit for two years. David Phelps had more to offer than just an American break. He was currently working on Ted

Kennedy's US presidential campaign. He knew if anything would induce Jane to take a holiday, the opportunity to work on a presidential campaign would. He was right. Jane had experienced a taste of Australian politics through her Uncle Peter, who was a Liberal MP in South Australia. On many occasions when she was working in Adelaide she had partnered him to official functions. She was also a paid-up member of the party and had been the secretary of the Young Liberals for a period of time. The chance of being involved in American politics, albeit on a very small scale, was certainly a major attraction. She spent two months working alongside David and hordes of others, opening mail, hanging posters, and inveigling the reticent American voters to place a tick alongside Teddy's name. It wasn't all hard work. Twice a week she and David would head to the Pentagon to play squash. 'David had a pass to get into the Pentagon and he would sneak me in. What struck me most was the lifts. When you got in you noticed there were no floor numbers or buttons. You had to punch in a code for where you wanted to go. I never knew what floor the squash courts were on, all the time I was there.'

During her two-month stay in America, Jane, her flatmate Jackie Hides and David made a visit to Ted's home base of Boston and were allowed to enter his personal office. 'It was a massive room with incredible memorabilia. I sat in his chair and we took photos of each other. There was an American flag in the corner; it was all very patriotic. And there were heaps of framed photos and framed letters from JFK and Bobby Kennedy. The aura around the Kennedy family back then was intense and to get into the inner sanctum was beyond belief.'

While she never got to meet the man face to face, her efforts on his behalf did not go unnoticed. Prior to heading back to New Zealand she was presented with a signed photo, 'To Jane, from Ted Kennedy', and a copy of a leather-bound book that Ted had written for the family comprising many of John's speeches. The book has since provided inspiration prior to many public-speaking engagements.

It must have seemed a bit of a comedown to be back working at her Waikanae cafe after the excitement of a US presidential campaign. But it wasn't the lack of political thrills that made her decide to sell Tootlebury's. Instead, it was the back-breaking aspect of the job. 'The consequence of being in the restaurant and lifting heavy trays, bending down to ovens all the time, was I damaged my back. Within eighteen months I was having to wear a back brace because I had caused so much damage. In the end I had to get out, because I was making myself really ill.'

So ill in fact that her weight plummeted to 7 stone (44 kg) and her predisposition to migraines was exacerbated. Even now, two decades on, she still suffers from the injuries incurred in those two short years as a cafe owner. It was a watershed period in her life, Jane admits. She knew she had to sell the cafe, but prior to doing that she had to find a job. Serendipity played its part in the form of a small advertisement in the jobs vacant column of the Wellington morning paper, the *Dominion*. Montana was advertising for a viticulturist to be based in Marlborough. Despite her earlier declaration that she would never work in the wine industry, a spark of interest was ignited. 'I thought, maybe I should go for this job.'

Montana Wines was New Zealand's largest wine company, with vineyards in Gisborne, Auckland and more recently in Marlborough. Since the first plantings in 1973, they had quickly come to realise Marlborough had the potential to become New Zealand's most significant wine-producing region. Although in all fairness, the development in 1973 almost never got off the ground. Those first plantings were a nightmare. The grapes first planted were actually only cuttings taken from the company's Gisborne vineyards. They had simply been uprooted and then stuck into Brancott Estate's dry, free-draining soil with no irrigation. Despite huge efforts from the staff, who watered them with a tractor-mounted water tank, 60 to 70 per cent of the vines died. Hundreds of local school children were brought on field trips to help cover the vines with waxed cones, to protect them from frost and wind. Over 800,000 cones were spread out across the vineyard, making the fields look more like something out of an alien movie than a conventional vineyard. The cones worked a treat, protecting the plants and helping to conserve moisture. The only problem was there was nothing to hold them down, so when the famous Marlborough nor'west wind arrived, it literally picked the cones up and sent them barrelling across the vineyard and up against surrounding fences. Twelve months later Montana replaced the dead vine cuttings with potted rooted vines from their Auckland nursery and wisely made the decision not to use cuttings again.

By the time Montana advertised for a national viticulturist, the Marlborough vineyards were ten years old. The potential was apparent and the company saw the need to have someone with experience on the ground in the region. While Montana had previously had a viticultural expert in the form of Wayne Thomas, the employment of a national viticulturist to oversee all the company's vineyards and growers was novel. Peter Hubscher, who would later go on to become the CEO of Montana (later to become Allied Domecq and then Pernod Ricard) and the Chairman of the Board of New Zealand Winegrowers, was the production director in 1982. He says the company was trying to lift the standards of what was happening in the vineyards, especially as so many of the contract growers had absolutely no vineyard knowledge. 'We had millions of dollars invested in those vineyards and I knew we needed to take the same approach as we had been taking in the winery. We would never have allowed an unqualified winemaker loose, yet we had [inexperienced] farmers caring for the vines. I was trying hard to lift the science of what we were doing in the vineyards; it was part of the growth of the company.'

Which meant that when Jane applied for the job, Peter was impressed with her background. 'She not only had grown up with grapes, as her father had a vineyard, but she was also very qualified. At that time there were very few people in New Zealand that had formal viticultural qualifications, so she stood out. The fact that there were very few women in the wine industry wasn't a problem. We decided to break the mould and employ her.'

Peter says Jane brought a raft of new skills and experience to the job, and a disciplined way of dealing with problems. 'All university graduates bring different ways of thinking and she certainly added to our pool of skills.'

Within weeks of applying for the job, Jane was preparing to head to Marlborough, a small province at the top of the South Island.

Chapter 3

Harmonious

*A wine term which describes all the elements of
the product coming together to form a balance*

Dry, windy and dusty conditions assailed Jane when she arrived in Marlborough in January 1983. The region was gearing up for the upcoming vintage and while locals were complaining heartily about the lack of rain and the enveloping heat, Jane was struck by how temperate the conditions were, compared with her home in South Australia's Riverland.

Throwing herself into the new role as national viticulturist, she was surprised at the lack of vines throughout the small Marlborough pocket. While Montana had originally bought just under 1200 hectares of land ten years earlier, they had since sold a large portion off, deeming much of it unsuitable for grapes, retaining just over

440 hectares. Besides Montana, there were only five other companies based in the Marlborough region. Te Whare Ra Wines run by Allen and Joyce Hogan was based on the outskirts of Renwick. Twelfth-generation Champagne maker Daniel Le Brun had arrived with his wife Adele to establish a French-style methode traditionelle winery, just down the road from the Hogans. And Ernie had recently established Hunter's Winery on Rapaura Road. Corbans had arrived in 1980, purchasing 300 hectares of land in the Rapaura area and Penfolds New Zealand Ltd, headed by Frank Yukich, the man who had had the foresight to plant the first grapes in Marlborough, had a number of contract growers.

Müller Thurgau was far and away the major variety planted. It yielded good crops, suited the region's conditions and was perfect for bag-in-box wines, the lifeblood of the New Zealand wine industry at the time.

It was a learning curve for Jane as she had never had any experience with Müller Thurgau as a variety. She also had to come to terms with the differences in climate in Marlborough, compared with what she had grown up with. 'In Australia the fruit gets sunburnt, of course, so you have to have the leaves covering the fruit. In Marlborough it's the opposite. You have to train everything up to let in the sun.'

Initially canopy growth was so vigorous that many of the vines would meet in the middle of the rows. Jane's role as national viticulturist for Montana saw her experimenting with differing trellising systems in an effort to decrease canopy growth and increase grape quality. While the majority of Montana's crop was Müller Thurgau, there was a small tract of the Brancott Vineyard that was devoted to Sauvignon Blanc. These rows had been planted east to west, which meant the fruit was ripening appreciably differently on each side. Jane suggested to Peter Hubscher they remove some of the leaves to allow even ripening. It was a laborious job, given it was done by hand. She wistfully mentioned to one of the company's engineers that if there was an appropriate machine the job could be achieved in one-tenth of the time it took by hand. The engineer, John Fairhall, took Jane's comments on board and within a few days had come up with a mechanised solution. 'It was a very basic fan that he had inverted and mounted onto a tractor. As he drove along between the rows, it sucked the leaves in and then cut them off. We said, "Well, that's pretty damn good".'

Kiwi ingenuity even solved the problem of the leaves being sucked back into the engine of the tractor and clogging it up. John draped a wet hessian bag over the engine, protecting it from the falling debris. It was an innovative answer to a time-consuming problem. The leaf plucker was fine-tuned over the next few years, before machinery giants Gallagher took it over and developed it further.

Jane's first vintage in Marlborough went smoothly. The weather stayed fine, the disease threat was minimal and the grapes were in good condition. It was a gentle introduction to the region. As national viticulturist, Jane spent a considerable amount of time travelling, particularly to Gisborne, where Montana had a large collective of contract growers. It meant she didn't have a lot of spare time to socialise in the ever-growing Marlborough wine circle. After five months in the job, she still hadn't met many industry personnel outside of the Montana camp. But her name and reputation was spreading. One person who was intent on meeting her was Ernie Hunter. He had secretly given her the moniker of Miss Montana, and openly discussed her many attributes, not the least her good looks, with friend Richard Bowling, who was working for Corbans at the time. 'I had had a bit to do with Jane while she was working at Montana. Ernie knew this and he would say to me, "Ah, Mr Bowling, are you happening to be having a look at Miss Montana?" When I told him no, he said, "Well if you don't mind, I might have a bit of a look myself." And away he went.'

It actually took five months for Ernie to find a reason to contact Jane. He was planning a wine tasting at the new winery, with special guest John Buck from Te Mata Estate in Hawke's Bay. He duly invited Jane to come along and, despite not being overly enthusiastic, she agreed to do so. It was June, the middle of winter, and one of the wettest months of the year when she drove out to Hunter's in Rapaura Road. In the damp darkness, she drove past the winery sign three times before finally finding her way up the drive, past the overhead trellised vines. Never one to do things by halves, Ernie had invited just about everybody he knew in the region. There were contract growers, lawyers, accountants and industry personnel all gathered in the small lounge of his homestead. Jane arrived a little later than everyone else and was not initially introduced to the host. Although she had never met Ernie, she had been told a thing or two about him by her workmates, and had a very clear vision of what he would look like. 'I had heard stories about him at work and I imagined him to be a kind of wizened-up little sugar daddy Irishman. It was later in the evening when Chris Rose asked me if I had met Ernie. I had been looking for this little leprechaun-like Irishman all night and hadn't spotted one, so I said no. She said that's him over there, and pointed Ernie out. I remember thinking, "Well that's not what I expected."'

The attraction was instant, once they were finally introduced. Chalk and cheese they may have been, but the two discovered they had an awful lot to talk about. 'We probably chatted away for a couple of hours after everyone else had left.'

Within a week of that first meeting, Jane's dad arrived from Australia, taking a break from his own vineyard. She took advantage of his visit to introduce him to Ernie.

The two men hit it off, although Brian was a little scathing about the Irishman's decision to sink all his money into a winery. 'I remember when we were getting into the car to drive away, Dad said, "Oh my God, what a fool. Who would want to be involved in a winery and grape growing these days? He must be crazy — I wonder if he knows what he is in for." Ernie must have overheard that, because the next day he sent me a bunch of flowers with a cryptic message in German. It was a quote, stolen I might add from Wolf Blass of Australia, which when translated loosely said: Whoever doesn't like wine, women and song, stays a fool for life long.'

The romantic notion behind the flowers was not what Jane had expected from Ernie. 'He had another side of him other than the gregarious side that most people got to see. He was quite a romantic and he was also a bit of a homebody. He loved being at home with no one around, and loved to cook. Good old Irish food mainly. In fact he would do trays and trays of food and there would just be the two of us. But then he had that side that a lot of Irish people have, when they have to burst out and have people around them.'

With Jane having to spend time in Gisborne with her job, and Ernie travelling to sell his wine, the pair didn't get to spend a great deal of time together. And there were very few in Marlborough who realised they had become an item. Both were aware their liaison could be misinterpreted, with Jane working for Montana and Ernie selling some of his grapes to rival company Penfolds. Initially they got together in Christchurch, where Ernie still had a base. But within months he wanted to formalise their relationship and asked Jane to marry him. 'We actually got married in May of 1984. Ernie would have been married much earlier if he had had his way, but I said we had to wait until after vintage.'

In the meantime, Jane concentrated on her work at Montana, encouraging the company and the growers to consider new technology. She introduced mechanical pruning, overhauled the vineyard's irrigation systems, encouraged aerial spraying and organised workshops on viticultural practices for the local growers.

As for Ernie, he was quickly discovering that life as a wine producer was not meant to be easy.

Unbeknownst to him, when he had purchased his twenty-six hectares in Rapaura, he was buying into one of the most anti-alcohol sub-regions in the province. Bill Walsh describes it as 'a bigoted area', where anything to do with wine was viewed as a sign of the devil. The Women's Christian Temperance Union was a force to be reckoned with and they regularly petitioned against the growing wine industry. Local grain and crop farmers were concerned that having a vineyard along their boundary would threaten their right to use chemical sprays and therefore their livelihood. Plus there were still many within Marlborough who viewed the wine industry as a five-minute wonder that would never last. It was into this cauldron of rural prejudices that Ernie threw his plans for promoting the region's wine potential. He had already established a small wine shop in front of the new winery. While it was little more than a shed, it managed to attract visitors keen to sample the Hunter's wines and meet the man behind them. Ever the salesman, Ernie encouraged all visitors to the shop to go onto his mailing list, after which they were regularly updated with newsletters and special offers. Developing this ensured Ernie an outgoing of wines, without him having to rely on distributors, who weren't knocking his door down to represent him. But Ernie believed there was an opportunity to attract even more visitors, if signs promoting the wineries were installed on major highways in and out of the region. Not everyone agreed with his simple logic. The anti-alcohol movement was against him. Then he struck a battle with the local councils, who believed winery signs were a traffic hazard, diverting drivers' attention away from the road. It's interesting to note that twenty-five years later, the Marlborough wine industry is still battling this dogma of opinion. But he was not one to give up. Together with Allen Hogan, Ernie devised a wine trail map that highlighted where the wineries were in the region. They were available from the local Information Office as well as motels, the Interisland Line Ferries and hotels. While the map wasn't overloaded with cellar doors, it was a positive step in the right promotional direction. From small beginnings, Marlborough's wine trail has grown, now encompassing more than forty-five cellar doors and many more visitor attractions. To further promote the growing wine industry, Ernie contemplated buying Barry's Hotel in the centre of Blenheim and turning it into a wine library. The only problem, according to friend John Hoare, was the lack of anything substantial to go into the library. His efforts at promoting not only his own winery but also the region were gaining Ernie a lot of local attention. Altruistically, he was sowing the seeds for the future; which was important, because he needed to increase sales and income. With interest rates still climbing, debts to be repaid and a shed full of wine, Ernie ended up hitting the road and calling in a number of favours he had with liquor retailers throughout the South Island. 'Ernie used to put cases of wine in the car and head off down South for two weeks at a time trying to sell,' Jane says. 'He had a lot of friends in the liquor industry and I think the only reason they bought the wine was because of Ernie. It was pretty cheap back then, in an effort to get people interested in it. Then he would head over to Wellington and walk the streets trying to get people to buy it. They were pretty awful times.'

Determined not to follow the path taken by the bigger companies in Marlborough, Ernie shied away from the bag-in-box wines of the day. He openly said the day he had to produce bulk wines was the day he would give up: 'That is the day the magic will be gone. We are staying at the top end of the market, because that is where the fun and excitement is.'

Financially he would have been better off if he had embraced the bulk wine mentality. He could have increased production and therefore profit. Instead, he stuck with his 'quality first' mantra and insisted on hand-pruning and hand-making the wines. In the long run his persistence would pay off. In the interim he was facing a severe cash flow problem.

While he was managing to get rid of a few cases through his travels round the South Island, and even more was leaving through the tiny onsite wine shop, sales weren't enough to generate the cash required to reduce the financial noose hanging round his neck.

The building of the winery had required a major capital output, and as interest rates continued to rise Ernie was forced to come up with a money-making scheme. He decided to capitalise on the public interest in the romanticism of wine. Advertising in the Sunday papers he offered consumers the chance to buy a vine in Hunter's vineyards. For $68 they would receive certification of their vine and a map outlining just where it was planted. On top of that, every year for the next five years the vine owner would receive a free bottle of the Winemaker's Choice.

The response was phenomenal, far better than even Ernie could have predicted. Hundreds of people sent their $68, and duly received their vine certificate. More and more of those vine owners began calling in to the winery to check on their very own spot in the vineyard, buying more wine from the wine shop on the way out.

Even now Jane receives letters from individuals keen to know if their vine is still producing. Unfortunately, phylloxera decimated much of Marlborough in the early 1990s and none of the original Hunter's vines remain. That doesn't mean the vine holders have been forgotten, with the company still sending them invites to special events held in the main centres.

The influx of cash was a welcome boon to Ernie, staving off the creditors for a short time, and the interest from vine owners threw another marketing initiative his way. He decided the winery should be capitalising on the influx of visitors by establishing a vineyard restaurant.

The on-site homestead offered the perfect environment. Being an old villa set in established grounds, it lent itself to becoming an outdoor venue for relaxed dining. All that was required was an oversized barbecue, a kitchen where food could be prepared and the establishment of one room within the homestead that could serve as a reception area where food could be ordered. The sunroom of the villa provided the perfect reception. A wall was constructed to close the rest of the house off and the room served dual purposes. Food could be ordered there and, with a doorway into the kitchen, staff could come and go without disturbing Ernie or Jane in the rest of the house. But Ernie had no intention of being tied to the oven in this new venture. John Hoare says he loved the idea of being the host extraordinaire, so long as he didn't have to be involved with the cooking. 'So he provided the steaks, and got people to barbecue them. He said, "You don't want to get caught overcooking someone's steak, we'll let them do that themselves."'

A massive barbecue was built just off the sunroom, looking more like a wishing well than an instrument for cooking. Gas fired, it had four separate hot plates, which could be heated up in an instant to provide space for dozens of steaks at a time. Two smaller barbecues, placed alongside the outdoor brick fireplace that helped provide warmth on chilly nights, were used for smaller groups. He even included a large Para swimming pool in the backyard, along with slides and swings for children, strongly believing the best way to attract adults was to provide entertainment for their children. Hunter's vineyard restaurant was the first of its kind in Marlborough and quickly gained a solid reputation. Over the next few years it would be the destination of nearly every visiting food or wine writer, with large numbers of events taking advantage of its unique setting. It would also serve as the venue for Jane and Ernie's wedding, on 4 May 1984.

Chapter 4

Crusher

*A machine used in the winemaking process that
bursts the grapes' skins to release the juice*

George Orwell's novel *1984* depicted a world of negative
utopia. For Ernie that prediction may have been
written for him — albeit not in a sense of an overpowering
police state.

While his personal relationship with Jane was going
from strength to strength, the business was in a parlous
situation. Early in the year he told the *National Business
Review* the writing was on the wall for the New Zealand
wine industry, unless it began to open up markets outside
of New Zealand. He was talking from experience, having
learnt the hard way that selling wine from the back of the
Range Rover wasn't a recipe for financial success.

There had been a dearth of accolades for the 1983

wines, which when combined with the over-capitalisation on the winery, meant debt repayment was a major issue, especially as interest rates had hit 28 per cent. Often described as a man ahead of his time, Ernie could see New Zealand just wasn't big enough to accommodate his ambitions. He had his vine owners, who were also becoming extremely loyal buyers of Hunter's wines, and he had a solid list of winery visitors. But the domestic market was not large enough to cater for the growth of the wine industry. There was only one way to increase sales — exporting.

Ernie began by targeting New Zealand's neighbour, Australia. Hunter's was the first Marlborough boutique winery to take part in the annual Expovin, held in Sydney. Ernie, full of Irish charm and marketing nous, was able to talk the talk with anyone who was prepared to stop and listen. One of those who did stop, and was captivated by Ernie's larger-than-life personality, was the late Len Evans OBE, later to become one of the best-known stalwarts of the Aussie wine industry. When he first met Ernie, Len was the head of Rothbury Estate based, ironically, in the Hunter Valley. The coincidence of name wasn't lost on Ernie, who instantly thought of a novel way of using it to his advantage. He suggested to Len they establish a trans-Tasman deal whereby Rothbury could promote their wines through Hunter's newsletters and, in return, supply Ernie with a list of all of Rothbury's mail-order clients. It was a tongue-in-cheek offer given that Rothbury's wines already had a good reputation in New Zealand. If anyone was putting themselves out it was Evans, as Hunter's wines were completely unknown in Australia. Despite the one-sided advantages, Evans agreed and before Jane knew it she was wearing her tongue out, licking stamps and envelopes as they sent hundreds of newsletters and mail-order forms to every one of Rothbury's clientele. Ernie was determined to make an impact and chose not to include his order forms with the established Rothbury's mail-out. Instead, he posted them from New Zealand, believing it would increase the value of the wine if customers received a personal letter from Hunter's owner, complete with a New Zealand stamp on the envelope. Given the reaction, it seems he was right. Initially he had expected his New Zealand clients to snap up the Rothbury reds, predicting a three to one order ratio in favour of the Australian giant. The reality was the opposite, with three containers of Hunter's wines sent to Australia and Rothbury sending only one to New Zealand. This promotion also led to a change in the look of the Hunter's label. One Australian customer wrote to Ernie asking if he had considered taking advantage of his surname, which had a proud heritage in Scotland. 'She asked if we realised that with the name Hunter we were able to use the traditional Scottish family crest. Up until that stage Ernie had been using a label he himself had made up so it was pretty basic,' Jane says.

Despite the fact Ernie was Irish not Scottish, he readily embraced the idea of having an official insignia on his wine. A letter was duly sent to the Hunter clan in Scotland explaining the winery creed and asking permission to use the crest. Once consent was given, Hunter's was able to include the crest on all labels and promotional material. Containing a dog and the Latin motto *Cursum Perficio*, the crest was highly appropriate. 'Everyone thinks the label was chosen by us because of the dog, given that we have until recently always had dogs at the winery. But it's actually the traditional Hunter symbol.'

As for the Latin motto, *Cursum Perficio*, it has two translations according to Jane, both highly appropriate. 'One is, The Course Is Complete, which is the older translation. The more modern version is I Start What I Finish.'

While attending wine shows in Australia Ernie didn't limit himself to the trans-Tasman deal with Rothbury. He also established a relationship with the Société de Vigneron, a former subsidiary of the Australian Diners Club Magazine, which supplied subscribers with cases of wine from boutique companies. It was a major coup for Ernie, as he would now be able to supply a range of wines to the Australian market on a regular basis. While it wasn't an immediate answer to his sales problems, it would prove to be a significant boost when, twelve months later, Hunter's sent 2600 cases of wines to the Société. The

Australian venture reiterated to Ernie the importance of looking offshore for markets if the business was to grow.

While sales were still uppermost in his mind, he had another issue clouding his vision — his marriage to Jane. Both could foresee a Herculean event if others got to know about it, so they decided to marry privately without telling anyone other than two witnesses. Jane asked Jo Deans, a girlfriend she had worked with in Wellington, to be her witness, while Eddie (Nod) Brooks from Ashburton was Ernie's friend on hand. 'We knew if we let people know, it would become an event to rival *Ben Hur*. His family would want to come out and then my family would need to come over. And then there were all the friends. It was likely to become a major logistical nightmare so we decided it would be better not to tell anyone. We got married on a Sunday and asked our friends round for drinks at the restaurant that afternoon. They all thought it was just a get-together, although most of them weren't surprised when we told them we had got married earlier in the day. Most were expecting it.'

Ernie's father was a little put out though, not because he hadn't been invited to the nuptials, but because Ernie's older brother Ian had got married a week earlier, also in secret. Jane says she wasn't affected by nerves on the day, although Ernie did enough pacing up and down the driveway for the both of them. In near-perfect conditions the pair took their vows in the lounge of the homestead well before the guests arrived for afternoon drinks. Despite their commitment to each other, Jane wasn't about to leave her full-time job. Her expertise in the vineyards was extremely helpful for Ernie but she had no intention of becoming a full-time Hunter's employee. Initially, the couple had kept their relationship secret, given the possible comments regarding conflict of interest. But as time had gone on, both decided it wasn't worth the hassle. Being a viticulturist, Jane had no part to play in Montana's winemaking or marketing decisions. Montana's management agreed. They weren't keen to lose her expertise or innovative ideas. Aside from all that, Jane couldn't afford to leave Montana, as hers was the only steady wage coming into the household.

'They were pretty awful times. We were financed to the hilt because of the winery and it was always under-capitalised. We had borrowed equipment, which meant it wasn't up to the job. The vineyards needed money spent on them, the marketing needed money and we just weren't making any.'

For the first time she began to see the worried side of Ernie. 'I used to say that you could tell whether we had money in the bank or not because of the clothes Ernie wore. He had his fatter clothes and his skinnier clothes, which he would switch between depending on how things were going.'

Skinny clothes for when things were financially tough, larger clothes for when things were on the up. The stress told on Ernie. As a chain-smoker and at times heavy drinker, he was often still awake in the early hours of the morning. 'He would spend nights pacing the floor when he couldn't sleep because he was worrying about things. Then there were the nights when he would wake up at three a.m. with a bright idea and would have to work on it then and there.'

One of those bright ideas was to promote Hunter's to businesses in Wellington, a short twenty-minute flight away from Blenheim. This was no mail-order promotion. Instead, Ernie began marketing Hunter's restaurant for business lunches as a viable alternative to the more 'staid' restaurants in the capital's city centre. For $104, a person could fly from Wellington to Blenheim, be collected by taxi, driven out to Hunter's, be shown the vines, enjoy lunch with a complimentary wine and be returned to the airport for a flight home, all in the space of a few hours. Or for those who were looking for a night away from home, he offered a Friday night special. For $129 you could fly from Wellington at 6 p.m., have dinner at Hunter's, receive a bottle of wine, be accommodated at a Blenheim motel, and fly home early Saturday morning. The audacity of the promotion was typical of Ernie's ability to think outside the square. While it could never be deemed a raging success, it did help to get the

Hunter's name and the restaurant facility recognised by the business community. The publicity was beginning to work in terms of patronage at the restaurant, which at this stage was only open during the summer months. John Hoare remembers one important visitor who turned up unannounced, just as he and Ernie were about to enjoy a bottle of Breidecker under the trees. It turned out it was the Israeli ambassador, who had decided to call in and buy some wine on his way to Nelson. Ernie decided it was too good an opportunity to pass up, so offered to put on a luncheon for him. At the time it was pre-harvest and the birds were making a feast of the company's grapes next to the winery. Bird scaring was an ongoing task during this period, with staff employed solely to fire shotguns above the vines to scare off the birds. John says they had been having a drink with the ambassador while cooking their steaks on the barbecue.

'Just as we were taking them off the barbie there was this almighty noise and a shower of shot came floating in and landed on everyone's plate. There was this deathly silence as everyone looked from their plate to Ernie and back to their plate. It only took a few seconds before Ernie turned to the Israeli ambassador and said, "Makes you feel at feckin' home, doesn't it?" The ambassador just burst out laughing, he thought it was a great joke.'

On another occasion early on in the restaurant's history, Ernie had to placate a busload of Japanese tourists who thought their days were numbered after another incident in the vineyards. As Montana's viticulturist, Jane had instigated overhead spraying, which was extremely popular in Australia. 'I used to say to the pilot, "Look, as you go over Hunter's would you mind dropping a spray on the overhead trellis", which was quite difficult to get at. I made sure he would ring Ernie to let him know it was going to happen, just in case there was anyone in the restaurant. This one day Ernie didn't get the message and all these Japanese tourists literally dropped to the ground in fright as the plane flew over the vines at an incredibly low level. We kind of decided after that it probably wasn't the best thing to be happening.'

The restaurant was beginning to attract more and more visitors, which had some drawbacks for Jane especially. Originally Ernie had lived in the homestead that now housed the restaurant. But when he and Jane married they moved into a small flat at the back of the winery. Jane says being in amongst the business wasn't good for anyone so the couple moved across the road from the vineyard, into a small old cottage. 'I remember one day I was driving along Rapaura Road on my way to visit a grower and I saw Ernie crossing the road with one of my plant stands and the fireguard from the house. He was getting the restaurant ready for the season opening. That was typical of Ernie, he would take our own personal items to make the restaurant look more homely. Then at the end of the season he would bring them all back again.'

By mid-1984 it became obvious to Ernie that he needed some financial assistance, so he approached the Development Finance Corporation (DFC). DFC was a government-owned corporation established to promote industries that could contribute to the economy and create employment. Raising funds offshore, in particular in Japan, the corporation would lend capital to a business venture. With interest rates so high many New Zealand companies were faced with near ruin, including Hunter's. Kevin Podmore was a lending analyst for DFC and inherited Ernie as a client in 1985, one year after Hunter's was given an export suspensory loan. 'This encouraged people to concentrate on exporting their product in an effort to increase earnings,' says Kevin. 'Ernie had to achieve certain sales hurdles and if he did so the government would write the loan off.'

But the loan wasn't enough to stave off the creditors or help the company progress with future developments. In 1985 Kevin was asked to put together a deal whereby Hunter's could borrow from DFC to tide the company over a major hiccup with finances. 'He needed working capital, so what we did was separate the vineyards from the operating business, which was the winery. We then injected some cash into the business, holding a 40 per cent share. The wine industry is very capital intensive and it just wasn't returning any sort of profit. For Ernie there was another problem, as he didn't want to sell his stock too early, before it was ready. With the investment from DFC he had the ability to hold wine stocks for a while until he could achieve sales.'

Despite the negative connotations of having DFC involved in Hunter's, Ernie never showed any pessimistic attitude to Kevin. 'He was always very positive and that was part of his charm. To him, borrowing wasn't a major issue if it allowed him to develop the company.'

Looking back at those times, Kevin says Ernie was always great fun to be around. So much so that his visits to Hunter's were always timed for the end of the day, as Kevin knew he wouldn't get away from Ernie in any short time-frame. 'He was always my last port of call when I was in Marlborough. He would ply me with drinks and I would have been useless to go and see anyone after that. But seriously, Ernie was great fun and I enjoyed doing business with him.'

Chapter 5

Grafting

Joining budwood and rootstock together

A hundred years before Ernie bought his Marlborough vineyard, German immigrant Heinrich Breidecker introduced grape growing in the far north of New Zealand. His name was later immortalised by the New Zealand Wine Institute when a Geisenheim Müller Thurgau cross clone was renamed as Breidecker. It was this variety that would play a large role in the formative years of Hunter's. Producing a sweet white wine, it was the perfect grape for Hunter's German-born winemaker Almuth to experiment with. It was also an ideal first wine to lure uninitiated drinkers.

Ernie had great faith in Breidecker and was known to scoff at Montana's promotion of Blenheimer, a medium white wine made from Müller Thurgau grapes. It is easy to see why the company was making the most of the name, especially when they erected a large billboard at the entrance to their winery site on State Highway 1 south of Blenheim welcoming visitors to 'Blenheimer country.' Always the public joker, Ernie threatened on more than one occasion to overwrite the billboard with 'Breidecker — Blenheimer's Favourite Drink!' Common sense prevailed; given Jane's position at Montana, this was just as well.

While not a fan of Müller Thurgau, Ernie was aware of its attributes as a quaffing wine. As an early-ripening, high-yield variety, it was something of a cash cow to wineries, especially those companies producing it in three-litre casks. Determined to avoid going down that path, Hunter's was releasing its Müller Thurgau as a quality bottled wine. The abilities of the variety even impressed Jane's father. He planted a small tract of Müller Thurgau in the Riverland in South Australia, which provided Ernie with a grand scheme. 'Because it matured earlier than it did here in Marlborough, Ernie wanted me to have it crushed and tanked over,' Brian says. 'His aim was to hit the market ahead of all his mates. He was deadly serious about getting it in and beating everyone else with a wine release.'

Although the idea was good, the execution was a little more difficult and the early release of a Hunter's Müller Thurgau never eventuated.

By now Ernie had been in Marlborough for five years

and the winery had been operational for three. More individuals were coming onto the scene as contract growers and the larger companies were starting to take notice of the fruit coming out of the region. Corbans had vineyards just down the road from Hunter's and the company winemakers were full of praise regarding the fruit quality. Dave Pearce (now winemaker for Grove Mill) was one of those who could see the writing on the wall. 'For us it was completely clear that the future of winemaking as we knew it lay in Marlborough. We were fortunate we had the direct comparison every year. We got about 500 tonne of fruit from Marlborough and we were doing up to 9000 tonne of Gisborne fruit. The consistency of flavour of the fruit from Marlborough was far better than the 9000 tonnes from Gisborne in almost all varieties.'

James Healy, who went on to become a winemaker with Cloudy Bay and now is part owner and winemaker for Dog Point Wines, agrees. 'I remember thinking the quality was so much better than anything I had ever seen until then.'

Yet despite the quality, the industry was suffering as a range of government initiatives began to take effect. In 1981 import licences were removed from wine to promote competition within the industry. Tax incentives that had encouraged a large number of individuals to plant grapes were starting to be phased out, which when combined with the ridiculously high interest rates were causing panic among growers and producers. Making matters worse, domestic consumption of wine was dropping, creating what was deemed a wine glut. An old-fashioned price war began, which given Ernie's history in the liquor industry he should have been prepared for. This time, however, it was Ernie on the receiving end and not the one dictating the terms. The major companies were desperate to get rid of their wine reserves, selling three-litre casks for as little as $8. Bottles of quality varietals were being sold for less than $3, hardly enough to pay the winery for the cost of production, let alone the grape grower. The pressure was being felt across the board, with larger companies such as Delegat's and Villa Maria–Vidal going into receivership. Penfolds New Zealand Ltd was unable to pay its growers for the 1985 vintage, being saved only when partner Lion Breweries came to the party and honoured the debts. Hunter's too was feeling the strain, which led Ernie in June 1985 to approach DFC for more capital. 'At that point Ernie could have taken the easy route and cashed up on his investment and walked away,' Jane says.

Instead, on DFC advice he divested himself of his liabilities by selling his vineyards and leasing out the restaurant. In return for the capital injection DFC took a 40 per cent share in the winery. 'Ernie was adamant the reason DFC put the high interest rates in place was because they wanted you to work hard and buy your bit back. As if we weren't already working hard. It was pretty cruel.'

The Hunter's-owned vineyards were sold off, one to a grape grower, the other to a deer farmer. The properties were sold without being advertised and Ernie ensured he had contracts with both purchasers, guaranteeing continuity of supply. The only vineyard the company retained was a two-hectare block behind the winery. Even the much-lauded restaurant was leased out, making the fiery Irishman see red. He angrily told a reporter that the situation was 'a brutal ploy by the big companies to put the little ones out of business'. To make matters worse, Almuth Lorenz, Hunter's winemaker since 1981, had given notice. She intended establishing her own winery in Marlborough although she promised to stay on until after the 1986 vintage. There wasn't much for Ernie to smile about during these dark times, although there was one bright note to come out — a major accolade for a 1984 wine. The Sauvignon Blanc won the 1985 New Zealand Easter Show Trophy for the Highest Points from a South Island Winemaker. After some less-than-complimentary reviews of his 1983 wines, this trophy helped buoy Ernie. There were other incremental steps forward. Earlier in the year the first official Marlborough Wine Festival had been held. A strong advocate of bringing together the handful of wineries to promote en masse to the media and public, Ernie at the last minute pulled out. One of his famous falling-outs with someone would have been the reason for his grand departure, although decades on no one can place a finger on just what brought about his change of heart. For someone who had been so adamant that a festival was a vital necessity, his actions can only be described as obtuse, especially since he had helped raise a large sum of money to get the event off the ground. Before selling his interest in Warner's Hotel in Christchurch, Ernie had acquired an astounding range of vintage wines, including some extremely rare French bottles. As Richard Bowling remembers with horror, those wines sat in cardboard boxes while the winery in Marlborough was being built.

'Some of the builders were helping themselves to bottles of Chateau Mouton Rothschild for afternoon tea. It was driving me nuts. I said to Ernie, "For Christ's sake, these are great wines, you shouldn't be keeping them in boxes for one thing and they shouldn't be left out for anyone to just grab hold of." So he asked me to catalogue them for him. Most were from the sixties and seventies and in 1984 Ernie auctioned them off to raise funds to develop a wine festival. Kingsley Wood came over and auctioned them and a lot of them went out the gate for a song. I could have cried. But to Ernie it was a publicity stunt. He raised funds for the festival because he could see the bigger picture and how a festival would benefit him.'

The February event was held to coincide with the opening of the publicly funded Marlborough Centre, in Blenheim's township. Te Whare Ra, Daniel Le Brun, Montana and Hunter's planned to open up their sites to visitors for tastings and entertainment. Penfolds and Corbans, who didn't have wineries in the province, were joining in establishing sites amongst the vineyards in Rapaura. Throughout the day visitors were able to travel by bus between the sites. At the last minute Ernie withdrew, choosing instead to invite a large number of wine writers to the winery itself, separate from the more public functions. Not that the public seemed to notice. The festival was a major success, with Montana running a beer hall theme complete with German steins (which wine was drunk from) and beer hall entertainment. Te Whare Ra had music and art on site and a tractor to run guests down to neighbouring Daniel Le Brun, while Penfolds had music and wine galore that tended to stop festival-goers in their tracks. Each site had personnel responsible for making sure festival-goers were continually moved on. Some of those involved in marshalling the crowds decided the party was just too good to work through, so they ditched their radio telephones and joined in. As a consequence there was a major backlog which saw other wineries further along the track missing out on some of the visitors. Ernie must have regretted not taking part, especially as he had been instrumental in the fundraising and the initial promotion.

French wine was not the only Warner's Hotel remnant Ernie retained when he left. He also had a quantity of old port that had apparently been sitting in the cellars of the hotel for years. Stewart MacPherson says it became the base for a Hunter's Port, released in 1985. 'It was under the original Hunter's label with Ernie's signature on it and was called a Cabernet Port. The label reads, "Twenty-year-old Oak Cellar Ports from around the world. Drawn from the late Barney Ballin's private cellar. Blended with our 1984 Cabernet Sauvignon and re-fortified. 750mls, 18.5% Alcohol."'

It's doubtful Ernie was expressing a desire to produce fortified wines with this release; more likely he was taking advantage of the government having lifted the sales taxes on sherries and ports by 54 per cent, in 1984. But not everyone was impressed with what was coming out of Hunter's winery. Montana's winemaker Peter Hubscher took Jane aside one day and offered some sage advice. If Ernie was serious about making a go of his boutique business then he should be looking closely at the quality of the product, the marketing of it and just where he was going to be able to sell it. 'He told me Ernie needed a good consultant if he was going to grow the business successfully. It was very good advice given neither of us had the winemaking skills required to take us up to the next level. The vineyards were my job, Ernie was marketing and Almuth was about to leave to set up her own winery. We needed someone to come in and give us an overview of the entire business.'

Ernie agreed and began recruiting internationally for a

consultant. He sensed he needed someone who had a feel for the international market, on top of the all-important winemaking advice. Ernie had just confirmed a major order with David Thomas from Cellar Master Wines in Australia — a direct mail company. The initial order was for 2500 cases of wine and was followed up with a subsequent order for 1500 cases. Because of David's knowledge of the international wine industry, it was him Ernie first approached for some potential consultant names. Top of the list was Tony Jordan, who was running Australia's largest wine industry consulting firm, Oenotec. He had a degree in physical chemistry and was a research scientist in the United Kingdom and United States before becoming a lecturer in wine chemistry and oenology in Australia. His consulting firm had a reputation for assisting in the rapid quality growth of many top Australian wineries. Meeting Tony for the first time, Ernie was impressed with his credentials. Not only did he have major skills in the production of wine but with his experience in wine promotion he had a real feel for the market. As for Tony, he has never forgotten that first meeting.

'My first impression of Ernie? An Irishman who had this beautiful way with words that could instantly enthuse you. He was extremely likeable and someone who could make you believe anything was possible. He was always thinking ahead and seemed to be two steps in front of everyone else, constantly seeing a bigger picture for his business. He was a salesman and an entrepreneur but he was also something of a dreamer. I got the feeling that he had a wide horizon to his entrepreneurial abilities.'

While the discussions took place in 1985, it wasn't until 1986 that Tony took up his role as consultant, just as Almuth left and the winemaking role became vacant.

Securing Tony invigorated Ernie and once again the marketing ideas began to flow. With his large order from the Société de Vigneron heading to Australia in May and the deal with Rothbury in the Hunter Valley, exports were picking up. With all the wheeling and dealing, finding a consultant, arranging export markets and promoting the wines, Ernie spent a considerable amount of time away from Marlborough. The ongoing administration fell on Jane during these times. Along with the sale of the vineyards and the leasing of the restaurant, staff numbers had dropped at Hunter's. There were no office staff, so it was up to Jane to manage the invoicing, basic accounts, wages and general correspondence. While it was prior to the introduction of Goods and Services Tax (which has created a whole new level of office administration), she says it was a trying time. 'Especially when Ernie decided that he needed a letter written. I'd often have to type them late at night, because he would come home and have to get it written there and then. We had this old typewriter and everything had to have a carbon copy, so there I would be with carbon and corrector ink and inevitably I'd get to the last sentence and make a mistake and have to start all over again.'

One of Ernie's major marketing ploys was the Hunter's newsletter, set up to coincide with the vine holders initiative. Every quarter the members would receive an order form for wine, a covering letter from Ernie and a newsletter containing snippets of information relating to Hunter's and other wine industry members. Ken Hudson, based in Christchurch, was commissioned to produce the information. All his articles were posted back to Hunter's and then Jane and Ernie cut and pasted the snippets onto a sheet suitable for photocopying. It was a mammoth task but given the ongoing orders for Hunter's wines it was a vital marketing tool. It also helped to elevate the position of one of Hunter's most endearing characters — Commodore.

It's appropriate that Ernie, a larger-than-life character, would choose a larger-than-life dog as his pet. Renowned for their size, St Bernard's are also loyal, loving and very friendly. Attracted to the presence of such an animal, Ernie bought his first St Bernard when he first moved to Marlborough, appropriately giving him the name of Pinot. The contrast in nature between the man and his dog was striking. Pinot was a gentle giant, unflappable, taking everything in his stride, when he could be bothered to be active. Ernie on the other hand was fiery, spontaneous and bristling with energy. Pinot was an integral part of the winery and a popular attraction for visitors. But his lack of road sense led to his death early in 1984. Devastated, Ernie and Jane decided it was too difficult to replace him. Six months later they received a call from a dog rescue organisation in Christchurch asking if they would adopt a St Bernard that had been mistreated. While both said they didn't want another dog, they were intrigued enough to travel to Christchurch for a look. 'We decided to go down, but we said to the woman that we were not really looking for another dog.'

They may not have been looking for a dog, but Commodore, who was eighteen months at the time, was certainly looking for another owner. Having been removed from a household where he hadn't been cared for properly, it appears Commodore knew how to recognise a couple who would provide him with a cushy lifestyle. 'We were talking to the woman who was looking after him and reiterating that we weren't there to pick him up, when she said, "Well, it doesn't look like you have a choice." Because there in the back of the car was Commodore, already settled in. He just wouldn't get out, no matter what we did. So in the end we brought him home with us.'

Commodore was to become an iconic feature of Hunter's, positioning himself right in front of the wine shop table to ensure he got as much attention as he possibly could. Visitors would be enthralled with his bulk and gentle nature and he was always being coerced outside for people to have their photo taken with him. 'He just loved it. He would sit there and throw his head back, lapping up all the attention. But as he got older he got a bit sick of all the fuss and would just walk away.'

The writer of Hunter's newsletter, Ken, established a regular Saintly Words column in the newsletter, where the dog's antics were highlighted in suitable doggy language. Before long Commodore was the best-known individual at Hunter's. Letters began arriving addressed to him. Presents were sent by fans all over the world and very few visitors to the winery or restaurant left without first having their photo taken with him. He was even included in significant events held at the winery. When Labour Trade Minister Mike Moore opened the winery extension in 1989, Commodore was included in the guest list. While he pretended to listen carefully to the Minister, it obviously became all too much for him. He pushed his way through the crowd and settled himself down in front of the podium where Mr Moore was delivering a rather long-winded speech. Tact not being a doggy trait, Commodore turned his back on the audience and promptly fell asleep, letting rip with thunderous snores. Mr Moore took the hint and abruptly ended his speech, claiming it was the first time in his political career that his ramblings had managed to send a dog to sleep.

Chapter 6

Flowering

*The beginning of the fertilisation process
that forms the tiny seed-bearing grapes*

While most people receive Christmas cards in the mail during the month of December, in 1985 contract grape growers throughout New Zealand were receiving letters telling them they had to dig up their grapevines. The first notification came on 22 December when Penfolds' growers were informed they had until the end of January to pull the vines out. Other growers in the province quickly discovered they weren't immune, when the announcement was made by the government that a vine pull was necessary to rationalise the burgeoning wine industry.

The aim was to cut New Zealand's vineyard area by a quarter, with growers to be paid $6175 for every hectare of grapes they removed. For many growers it was the last straw. They had faced ever-increasing interest rate rises, soaring fuel prices and a diminishing consumer market; now they had to turn around and remove what for many was their main source of income. While the price paid per hectare may have looked good on paper, it didn't take into account the cost of getting contractors in to do the job or the loss of production for growers. Giving a subsidy to the growers was also a bone of contention within the community; the feeling of town versus country was never more highlighted than during this period of uncertainty. The percentage of grapes required to be pulled depended on what the wine company's ratio of sales to production was. Wineries who were successfully selling their wine removed fewer vines than those whose wine was still sitting in the warehouse. Penfolds were hardest hit, with some Marlborough growers being asked to remove 100 per cent. Discussions saw Penfolds retract their instruction, with some growers getting away with having to remove 15 per cent, others having to remove 33 per cent. Corbans growers pulled out less and Montana less again — due to their wine sales being the highest of the three companies. What the government didn't foresee with their grand plan was that some growers would remove their grapes, take the money and then replant with quality varietals virtually the next day. One group of Marlborough growers was adamant they weren't about to remove any vines they had lovingly planted and nurtured, regardless of how much money they were offered. Instead, they leased a frost-prone vineyard, pulled out every single vine and used that to satisfy their quota. Many within the wine industry today view the vine pull as one of the most significant events in the development of Marlborough as a wine-growing region. It gave growers and wine companies a chance to take a breath and re-evaluate what they wanted in the future. It had become abundantly clear that New Zealand could never compete against Australia as a bulk producer. This country had to create a point of difference if it was to succeed on the world market. Instead of bulk, wine companies had to strive for quality, with varietals that consumers wanted. During the vine pull, nearly 189 hectares of grapes were pulled out in Marlborough, mainly Müller Thurgau, (Rhine) Riesling — ironically to make a comeback a decade later — and Gewürztraminer.

With their vineyards now sold, Hunter's had no vines to pull out, which in itself was a bonus. But the company's growers, including the two who had bought the vineyards off Ernie, were affected. In the latter's case they removed six-year-old Müller Thurgau plants and replaced them with Chardonnay and Sauvignon Blanc, providing Hunter's with even more commercially acceptable varietals. For Jane the vine pull was a busy time, especially as she was the main point of contact for Montana's contract growers in both Marlborough and

Gisborne. At this stage Gisborne was Montana's grape-growing hub, which meant Jane was constantly travelling out of Blenheim. The trips away had become more regular due to the advent of phylloxera, a sap-sucking louse that feeds off the roots of vines. While initially there are few signs of the disease, phylloxera eventually impacts on the vines' ability to produce, particularly in times of stress. There is no cure and the only solution is to remove the affected vine and replant with resistant rootstock. While it had been discovered in northern vineyards, Marlborough had managed for years to halt the spread south. In 1982 an aerial survey was undertaken by the Marlborough Grape Growers Association to see if there were any signs of the disease among the region's vines. At that stage there was none. In an effort to keep it that way, the Grape Growers Association began lobbying to ban the importation of grapevines from nurseries in the North Island. Even household grape plants were targeted by the Association, which caused considerable consternation among the wine-propagating nurseries in the country, all of which were based up north. All the efforts proved ineffectual; inevitably the disease was discovered in Marlborough in 1984, at a Penfold grower's vineyard near Montana's winery site at Riverlands. It was a devastating blow for the industry as a whole and a death knell for the poor grower. 'He was treated like a pariah by just about everyone,' Jane says.

For those growing for Penfolds there was an immediate backlash, with other contract growers not wanting to share equipment if it had been to the Riverlands site. It was a panic mentality that reverberated throughout the small growing community. Jane had already experienced the effects of phylloxera in Gisborne. Growers there were suffering far more from the disease as it had taken a stranglehold over large tracts of vines in a short period of time. It was a difficult time for Montana's growers in the region, Jane says, as they not only had to cope with the economic effects of phylloxera, which inevitably meant having to remove vines, but also with the necessity to change varieties away from the bag-in-box Müller Thurgau. But worse was to come, when in 1986 Montana bought out Penfolds New Zealand Ltd, giving them a 40 per cent share of the New Zealand market. Montana not only bought the wines of Penfolds but also the contracts with hundreds of growers, who weren't happy with the turn of events. 'It got very nasty at this stage, especially with the Penfolds' growers, who had very advantageous contracts.'

Those contracts were basically lifetime agreements lasting for ninety-nine years. Montana may have been happy to have a wider pool of growers supplying them but there was no way they were prepared to be in the former ninety-nine-year contract, which they thought would give all the power to the grower. Battle lines were drawn and endless discussion ensued as each side tried to force the other to give way. Jane was heavily involved in the negotiations as Montana's chief viticulturist and describes it as one of the darker periods within the wine industry, resulting in some fierce clashes. The growers were uniting together in an attempt to force Montana to pay an across-the-board payment for grapes, regardless of which region those grapes were coming from. Given the number of growers, it was a powerful lobby. But Montana was not about to back down either, despite the fact they needed the supply. In the end the Commerce Commission settled the argument by stating that the stance taken by the growers was anti-competitive and Montana was within its rights to nullify all contracts, which is what it did. Growers all of a sudden were treated as individuals rather than being part of a collective group. It was a new experience for everyone. Growers had to make a decision whether to re-negotiate with Montana or look for another wine company, such as Nobilos, Babich or Corbans. It was an acrimonious time and years later people describe it as a bitter, almost personal, battle, rather than a confrontation of business ideology. Regardless of how it was viewed at the time, the result of the Commerce Commission decision changed the face of New Zealand's wine industry. It provided the impetus for a number of small companies to establish themselves in the Marlborough region. It also allowed wine companies to begin rewarding growers for quality, which in turn led to superior wines.

Somewhat insulated from these events, Ernie was still conjuring up audacious marketing ploys. Buoyed by the sales to Australia he began thinking further afield. As a son of Ireland he was well aware of the United Kingdom's penchant for wine and strongly believed his wines would appeal to the British palate. He discussed the prospect of exporting to the UK with Australian David Thomas from Cellar Master Wines, who suggested Ernie needed to get his wines into the public domain in England and bring them to the notice of retailers, consumers and the media. The Sunday Times Vintage Festival, held annually in London, would be the ideal venue, if the organisers could be convinced to give wines from New Zealand a showing. Knowing the organiser, Tony Laithwaite, David made the first approach. Tony had already visited New Zealand and had met Ernie after flying in to Marlborough, an occasion he still remembers. 'The plane from Wellington dropped me, the only passenger, at a bare airfield that only had a tiny little shelter. I waited and waited and was getting quite cross. Eventually a four-by-four hurtled up in a cloud of dust. Out stepped Ernie, a big man, huge smile, non-stop charm.'

The only other New Zealander he has been able to liken Ernie to is Jonah Lomu, whom he met twenty years later. He describes both men as 'big, charming and unstoppable Kiwis'.

Once Tony tasted the wines from Hunter's he had no

hesitation in inviting Ernie to submit three — the Fumé Blanc (an oak-aged Sauvignon Blanc), Chardonnay and Sauvignon Blanc, all from the 1985 vintage. 'It only took one sip for me to realise these wines were in a different league.'

The Sunday Times Vintage Festival is a major event, held over one week. In 1986 there were 350 pre-selected wines representing thirteen countries. Just being there was a major boost to Ernie. He was fair bristling with excitement at the promotional potential, particularly when thousands of individuals would be passing by his stand during the festival week. A panel of experts under the chair of renowned wine writer Hugh Johnson judged all 350 wines, prior to public tastings. Those tastings involved 6000 members of the Sunday Times Wine Club, who over three separate sessions got the chance to swirl, sip and spit their way through all the wines. For many it was a case of identifying new releases for restaurant lists or fine trade retail. Others were looking for wines to purchase at a later date. And prior to leaving, all 6000 were asked to name their favourite wine. Being in the company of some of the greatest wine producers in the world didn't faze Ernie. It just made him more determined to make an impression. To ensure his stand and his wines weren't overlooked, he supplied trays of fresh oysters to accompany the tastings. With tongue in cheek he told everyone he had flown them in by Concorde from Bluff, at the very bottom of New Zealand's South Island. He had in fact bought them from a tiny store right in the heart of London, but it wasn't Ernie's style to let the truth stand in the way of a good marketing story. In some ways it was unfair to unleash him on the world of wine in an environment like this. There was no way anyone could compete with his unbridled passion and enthusiasm. With an oyster in one hand and a bottle of wine in the other, he would target anyone walking by. It was impossible not to be lured in by his eloquence and charm. What's more the wine was good — and so were the oysters. The end result was exactly what Ernie had hoped for — public acclamation. On the final night of the event the winners of each category were announced. Much to the French exhibitor's fury, Hunter's Fumé Blanc 1985 was awarded a gold medal for the best non-Chardonnay full dry white wine of the show. Then came the announcement of the favourite wine of the show, as judged by three separate groups of club members. The first group chose Hunter's Fumé Blanc. Then the second group also chose Hunter's Fumé Blanc. That in itself created quite a stir, given that only once in the twelve-year history of the competition had two different sessions chosen the same wine as the best. When the third session winner was announced, Ernie was on tenterhooks. First the officials announced the third most popular wine, then the second. When Hunter's Fumé Blanc hadn't been placed in either of those two positions, the hall full of 5000 people began chanting, New Zealand, New Zealand. Sure enough, Ernie had achieved an unheard-of hat-trick, being voted the best wine of the show by the third session of 2000 club members. It was a popular win, due mostly to Ernie's indomitable personality and the way he had passionately extolled the virtues of New Zealand wines. But, in a laid-back manner, Ernie hadn't considered the dress code of such a prestigious event. With boyish charm he strode on stage to collect his trophy, not in black-tie regalia, but wearing a classic New Zealand Canterbury rugby-style jersey, which must have been galling to the more elite wine producers present. How had this unknown Irishman, from the bottom of the world, managed to usurp the place of the world's most renowned winemakers? There were some aghast faces amongst the French contingent and protests were lodged. First the French claimed that under the EEC regulations a permit had to be granted for the name Fumé Blanc to be used on a label. What made this such a petty protest was the fact that the French did not complain about Australian and Chilean wines that were also labelled Fumé Blanc. When that protest was overruled, they protested on the grounds that the wine was not commercially available at the time in Europe. Again the objection was overruled. For Ernie, the protests and objections were just another indication that he had rattled the best in the world. He never missed an opportunity in the following media hype to impishly point out the unsportsmanlike attitude of the French. 'They were so childish and petty. They were lucky not to get a punch on the nose from me.'

With Ernie floating from his success and imbued with a good dose of Irish whiskey, Jane could hardly make out what he was talking about when he rang her. 'He was just babbling really, he was on such an immense high. I mean, this is the guy from Belfast who came out to New Zealand and then went to London with some wine and won the biggest prize of all. It was incredible. He had had such a relaxed attitude to the whole event, which is obvious when you see he is dressed in Canterbury apparel. But he had the personality to pull something like that off.'

The accolades for the wine began to flow. Hugh Johnson described it as 'having the golden gooseberry flavours of an exceptional Loire vintage. Lovely cleanness and bright oak gives the Fumé Blanc a softer, broader flavour.'

Another of the judges, Serena Sutcliffe MW, said: 'The big discovery of the show was the wine produced by Ernie Hunter in New Zealand. The intrinsic quality was truly remarkable — it is a tremendous find.'

While the Fumé Blanc was gaining all the attention, it wasn't the only wine from Hunter's to be noticed. The 1985 Chardonnay was also creating waves. Hugh Johnson told Ernie it had been very difficult choosing between the two wines, as the Chardonnay was of equal standing to the Fumé Blanc. 'It is on the scale of a Burgundy Premier

Cru.' Both the Chardonnay and the 1985 Sauvignon Blanc were awarded medals. Three wines, three medals and one trophy. Ernie had hit the big time and he was now inundated with orders. Having won the trophy, the Fumé Blanc was automatically included in the Sunday Times Wine Club dozen offered to members via mail order. In what was a follow-on coup, Hugh Johnson, the president of the Wine Club, offered Ernie a one-off chance to write to the club members promoting his other wines. Hugh prefaced Ernie's letter with one of his own.

'An unknown young New Zealander took this year's Club Vintage Festival by storm. He became the first person to score a hat-trick with the Members' Vote in all three sessions. Meanwhile the professionals upstairs gave him gold for his Fumé Blanc and silver for his Chardonnay.

'Under the circumstances the committee decided to do what we have never done before: to let the champion make his own offer of wine direct to club members. We just think that this is an historic moment for New Zealand's young wine industry which members will not want to miss.'

It was a marketing dream for Ernie, who wasted no time in dispatching letters to every Wine Club member offering a choice of two six-packs of wine. One was Breidecker, which he described as Hunter's biggest seller. 'It is one of the newest and most exciting wines to come from New Zealand,' and cost only £26.50 a case. Then there was the mixed half dozen: a bottle of Sauvignon Blanc, Chardonnay, (Rhine) Riesling, Gewürztraminer, Traminer/Riesling and Müller Thurgau at 'a never to be repeated price of £29.95 a case'. In total Hunter's sold 2000 cases of wine through the Sunday Times Wine Club, an amazing one-eighth of the entire production.

It wasn't just the English who were rushing in to buy Hunter's wines. An American was so enamoured of the Fumé Blanc that he wanted to buy the winery. When Dr Edwin Fondo, President of Exquisite Tasters International, was told it wasn't for sale, he offered instead to buy the entire production. In the end he had to settle for just two containers of wine. The audacity of Dr Fondo wasn't lost on Ernie or Jane. Suddenly they had gone from near bankruptcy to being the most sought-after winery in New Zealand.

CEO of the New Zealand Wine Institute at the time, Terry Dunleavy, says the win propelled New Zealand, and Marlborough in particular, onto the world stage. He describes Ernie's greatest attribute as being able to promote not only his own wines but the wines of the country. 'He was hugely important because in many places but especially in London and New York he was the first identifiable Marlborough and New Zealand wine personality that locals, trade and wine media encountered. When he spoke of his wine and of Marlborough he spoke with passion and commitment as if there was no other place in the world quite like it and indeed no other wine quite like his.'

Articles about Marlborough began appearing in illustrious wine magazines. Hunter's Chardonnay made *Decanter*'s Best Wines List in 1986 and the Fumé Blanc was awarded four stars in Australia's prestigious *Winestate* magazine. When Cloudy Bay's Sauvignon Blanc appeared in the UK a short time after Hunter's win, the media and critics began seriously taking note of what New Zealand was doing. The publicity meant that for the first time Hunter's was unable to supply everyone who wanted their wine. Jane says it was a complete reversal of the situation twelve months earlier. 'When Ernie came home he got a lot of television and media exposure. People kept ringing us up and wanting to place orders. They would complain if they couldn't get the wine, that we were selling it all overseas. But it wasn't that at all. It became a matter of allocating everything we made and invariably we would sell out very quickly.'

Things were starting to look up at Hunter's.

Chapter 7

Bottle shock

*A temporary condition of wine which often occurs
after bottling or when wines are shaken in travel*

When Ernie first bought land in Marlborough there
were only a few grape growers in the region. By
1987, though, the situation had changed dramatically.
Despite interest rates, vine pulls, company mergers and
contract renegotiations, the lure of the wine industry was
attracting individuals from all walks of life. Given that the
bottom had fallen out of the market for sheep, barley and
wheat, traditional farmers were looking for other means
of generating income. The end result was that more land
was becoming available for vineyards.

Marlborough is a unique region in terms of grape
growing. It has a distinctive synergy of climate and soil,
perfectly positioned at 41.3° South. In terms of age the

soils are young, approximately 14,000 years old, and vary throughout the many valleys of the region. Hunter's winery is set in the middle of the Wairau Plains and the vineyards surrounding it boast a range of fine alluvial silts through to stony gravels. One of the greatest attributes Marlborough offers is the significant diurnal temperature range, commonly a ten-degree difference between the heat of the day and the cool of the night. Constantly high sunshine hours through the summer and autumn period allow grapes a lengthy period to ripen slowly, ensuring that flavour components aren't lost or burnt off. Very much a cool-climate region, it suits varieties such as Sauvignon Blanc, Chardonnay, Pinot Noir and aromatics such as Riesling and Gewürztraminer.

By 1987 the producing hectares of Marlborough had increased considerably. There were now hundreds of hectares of grapes and even more was being planted. Outside companies were contemplating this part of the world as a viable alternative to Gisborne and Hawke's Bay. Still, the number of wineries within the region was small: Hunter's, Te Whare Ra, Daniel Le Brun, Cloudy Bay, Vavasour, Merlen, Montana and Corbans.

The 1987 Wine Festival was a chance to capitalise on what was happening in Marlborough and promote the wines to a growing domestic market. In the two years since the festival had begun, word had spread. The numbers attending the event in 1986 had astounded organisers and created major problems with transportation. It was decided that the best way to promote the wines was to congregate on one site. Montana offered their Brancott Estate Vineyard, an offer readily taken up by organisers. Set on the outskirts of Blenheim, Brancott was the first vineyard to be planted in Marlborough in 1973. Providing a natural mini amphitheatre dotted with trees and bounded by vines on one side and a small stream on the other, Brancott offers plenty of space for wine stands and food stalls. In its inaugural year, bales of straw provided seating while empty wine barrels stood sentinel for glasses to be rested on. The 1987 festival had a country fair atmosphere, with wine being sold by the glass and an array of local produce available for purchase. Mussels, fish, corn on the cob, even garlic ice-cream were on site to tempt the hungry or daring. One of the organisers of the event, Bill Floyd, says it showed a maturity not seen previously: 'I sensed some sort of French thing that I had never experienced in New Zealand before. We could have been sitting in Provence.'

It was a vindication of Ernie's plea for the industry to unite together to ensure future success.

The Wine Festival was just one of many promotional tools Ernie was utilising to ensure Hunter's increased its market share. But the problem with promotion and marketing is it takes time and effort and an inevitable increase in workload. It meant the couple hardly saw their slice of paradise set in the Marlborough Sounds. The bach in Penzance Bay, ninety minutes' drive from the winery, had provided many hours of solitude when both wanted time out from the rigours of the job. Set among beech trees teeming with birdlife and looking out onto the tranquil waters of the Marlborough Sounds, it offered the perfect retreat. The simplicity of the bach was far removed from the hectic lifestyle both were experiencing at work. Jane says it was an environment where the gentler side of Ernie came to the fore. He didn't have to keep up an image or be the life of the party when he was at Penzance; he could just relax and be himself. Quiet walks with Commodore, fishing off the jetty, wine and simple meals around the fire were revitalising. Inevitably, though, Ernie would return to the winery with a few more far-fetched ideas that he would want to put to his associates. But with the wines taking off, cosy weekends at the bach were getting harder and harder to fit in. Even the dinghy *Bounty*, which had sat at the winery throughout the winter, didn't get a chance to be taken off its trailer in the summer of 1987.

As Jane was busy preparing for the upcoming vintage, Ernie was getting ready for marketing trips overseas. In 1987 he travelled to Australia, and had two trips to the UK and one to the USA. The resulting sales were helping to pay back the borrowings that had amassed since the winery was built in 1983, although Ernie was quick to point out to the media that things weren't completely rosy. 'We are carrying forward a colossal loss since we started but at least we will be breaking even this year, which in view of what is happening in the industry means we're pretty lucky.'

Once again Hunter's wines were entered in the London Sunday Times Vintage Festival held early in April. Having just returned from one of his many trips, Ernie was back on a plane heading for London with two wines, the 1986 Chardonnay and the Fumé Blanc from the same year. Up against 380 wines from ten countries, he knew he had some stiff competition. There was no expectation that his coup of the previous year would be repeated, although Ernie was hopeful of picking up at least one medal. Instead, he collected two of only twelve golds awarded. This remarkable win was surpassed only when the Chardonnay was voted best wine of the show by the thousands of Club Members who had been cajoled to taste it. Show organiser Tony Laithwaite says it was a first for the competition. 'No one at the time had ever won so consistently.'

Wine shows may be de rigueur these days but in 1987 they were the lifeblood for emerging wineries. Being able to take part in one of the most prestigious wine events in Europe was an achievement in itself; winning the top award twice and being awarded three gold medals in two years was nothing less than a coup. Within a week the

Chardonnay was also being lauded in the USA, where it won a gold medal at the New York International Wine Show. Again Hunter's didn't have enough stock to satisfy demand from buyers in the States and Europe. With a significant portion already committed to Britain, Ernie had to make the decision to pull out of the Australian market.

Those award-winning wines were the very first created by a new-look winemaking team. Almuth Lorenz had left Hunter's straight after harvesting of the 1986 vintage. Tony Jordan was on board as consultant and one of his first tasks was to engage a new winemaker to replace Almuth. One of the first to apply for the job was John Belsham, who was working for Matua Valley Wines in Auckland. He knew Ernie, having shared a room with him at a Sydney trade fair some years prior. Matua Valley owner Ross Spence had made an off-the-cuff comment to Ernie not to get any ideas about stealing his winemaker, just because they were sharing a room. At the time of the comment, Ernie had no need for a winemaker, but a few years down the track he was more than interested in John's credentials. He had worked for a small wine company in France for five years prior to coming back to New Zealand to work for Nobilos and then Matua Valley. After interviewing John, Ernie suggested Tony should spend some time with him. The end result was that John was offered the job and arrived in Marlborough at the very beginning of 1987. His first impressions of the wines he had to work with weren't positive. 'They hadn't been finished and only some wines had been bottled. I finished bottling everything else that was suitable, but some of the wines were unsalvageable.'

Having Tony as a backup was one of the reasons John was so keen to get the job as Hunter's winemaker. He knew of his reputation as a consultant and once he met him personally he knew they could work together to make the most of the strong varietal characters that were present in Marlborough's fruit. 'Tony and I worked collaboratively on a few concepts that no one else was doing at that time. What we were doing would be considered fairly basic winemaking now, but back then it was quite revolutionary. We knew we had this wonderful fruit and it was our job as winemakers to present that in its purest form in the bottle. We embraced technology that had been prevalent in Australia for ten years but had only just started being used in New Zealand.

'The normal winemaking procedure of the era was to ensure skin contact with white wines, in an effort to extract flavour. Well, we canned that completely. We did no skin contact. Instead, we allowed the pure expression of the fruit to come through. That was quite revolutionary. Then because of Tony's background in premium white wine production in Australia, he understood the technology of low oxygen handling. I lapped it all up. Being able to tap into all that knowledge gave us a jump on all the other producers of the time.'

Tony, along with Jane, was pushing the mantra that good wine is made in the vineyard, which ensured John had the best possible fruit to deal with. But Tony wasn't just offering advice. He was also a hands-on asset when it came time to blend the wines. Jane says he is like a veteran sports commentator who can remember who passed the ball to whom, from a game played sixteen years ago. 'His palate is incredible. He can taste something and say, "Now go back and put five parts of this with ten parts of that and two parts of that" — it is an art. He remembers every component of each barrel and has an ability to know how to utilise those components to make a superb wine.'

The winery itself was undergoing some major changes thanks to Tony and John's involvement. As the company had been operating on a shoestring for so many years, the equipment was pretty dilapidated. John says the building had merit as it was insulated and had reasonable space, but the plant, while adequate, wasn't great, especially with all the second-hand equipment. The two men began working from the floor up to redesign the winery layout, equipment and procedures. The partnership between them was extremely strong and their teamwork helped propel Hunter's wines into a new league. But Ernie, while ecstatic to have someone of Tony's ilk on the payroll, was never overly comfortable in his presence. Jane says he was always in awe of him. 'He always felt that he didn't have the winemaking background or the credentials to converse with him. He really admired what Tony could do for Hunter's but I think he felt a bit inadequate. Whenever we were at something together, Ernie would make me sit next to Tony because he knew that I had the background to converse with him. It was one of those rare sides of Ernie that most people never saw.'

Despite the lack of winemaking credentials, Tony had no doubt about Ernie's many other skills. 'He was a huge leader in the whole emergence of Sauvignon Blanc in New Zealand. He had great belief in their ability to succeed and was one of the pioneers. He spotted the potential of Marlborough very early on and that was a stroke of genius.'

With export orders on the up, a new winemaking team and international acclaim, Ernie had some freedom to begin developing other aspects of the winery site. His great goal was to build an all-inclusive visitor village. With a restaurant and wine shop, the next obvious step was to provide accommodation. He began studying other such venues, particularly in the more established regions of Australia. Brian Arnold says that once again he was leading the field. 'He wanted to be the first in Marlborough to have a motel as part of the winery complex. They had spent a lot of time in the south of Adelaide, in the grape-growing areas, seeing what had been achieved in terms of restaurants and motels at vineyard sites. Ernie was convinced this was the next step in the evolution of the Hunter's name.'

He was also contemplating expanding in terms of wine varieties, expressing a wish to create a Pinot Noir 'beyond human understanding'. This was not because he had any particular love of the variety but he had seen the high prices French Burgundies could command and, having taken the French on with his Fumé Blanc, he felt confident he could do the same with Pinot Noir. Although, Jane says, there was a more practical reason for wanting to produce a high-quality Pinot. 'In the restaurant market in Europe, the UK and Asia, they always ask for a white and a red wine, especially for restaurant wine lists. We had been playing around with Cabernet Sauvignon and Merlot and we had this Pinot Noir as well. It was probably perceived as being more suitable for the area than the other two varieties.'

It was at this stage the Hunters began looking at buying a home of their own, something they could renovate together. Ernie had seen the perfect place not too far from where his friend Bill Walsh lived. 'I remember he turned up here one night and asked me who owned the old cob cottage in Renwick. I couldn't quite place it, but said I would find out for him. Before I knew it they had bought the place and were preparing to do it up.'

It certainly needed some doing up. Cob cottages, which

date from the mid-1800s, were constructed out of a mixture of clay and tussock, moulded together to form a cement-like formation. The cottage Jane and Ernie were looking at had been rented out and was in a derelict state. Some of the rooms had been shut off because there were no floorboards or the ceiling was falling down. Even to look at it wasn't a pretty picture. It had been painted bright blue, which while not exactly in keeping with the character of the era, had saved the cottage from total destruction. With no gutters, every time it rained the water literally poured down over the cob, Jane says. 'The paint saved the water from creating great gouges, thankfully, so the cob was still in pretty good condition. We knew, though, that a lot of work would be required as it hadn't been taken care of. It was an absolute hovel if I am truthful. There was this double-sided dung fireplace which was in good condition, but because of the fires all the ceilings were black. We had to get them scraped back, and discovered this beautiful cedar tongue and groove. There was borer in the floorboards and rooms without floors at all. But if you pictured it painted white and done up, it reminded us of farmhouses in Ireland and Australia.'

They asked Bill Walsh to put the offer in on their behalf, knowing that every other time they had looked at buying a house the real estate agents had seen dollar signs before their eyes and the price consequently rose. The offer was accepted and in May, Jane and Ernie were proud owners of a rather derelict hundred-year-old house, just minutes from the winery. With a trip to Adelaide planned for June, they began compiling a list of fittings and fixtures they needed to shop for.

But before they could take the trip, Ernie wanted to be sure he would come home to something a little more secure in terms of the company. He made the decision to take back control of Hunter's. Happy with the contract growers, his emphasis was on retrieving the 40 per cent share DFC held in the winery, Jane says. 'He went to them and said, "Look, there is no future in this business for you guys. You aren't going to make any money out of it and I am going to offer you this amount to buy the shares back." They looked at it and probably agreed there was no future for DFC in a small winery in Marlborough and they bailed out.'

Ernie signed the papers the day before he and Jane flew to Australia for their much-awaited break. It was one of only a few the couple had taken together. While Ernie would inevitably want to sell wine, Jane was looking forward to meeting her three-month-old nephew, James, her sister Libby's first-born child. The two-week break began in Tasmania, an area Jane wasn't enthralled about visiting. Ernie had travelled there once for a wine show and was quite taken with it, which to an Australian like Jane was strange. 'It really had nothing to recommend it at the time. It was going through some bad times and I remember driving to the bottom of the island where all these apples were being pulled out. I think there were a couple of vineyards there, but we didn't visit them. I'm not sure why Ernie was so adamant he wanted to go there.'

Melbourne was more to Jane's liking, and the couple spent two days there before heading to Adelaide to catch up with family. Ernie had no problem spending time with Jane's sisters, their partners or her father. On the contrary, he looked forward to the inevitable get-togethers. While he had stayed in touch with his family back in Ireland, he was not particularly close. On his trips to London for the Sunday Times Vintage Festival he surprised Jane by not making the short trip back to Belfast to catch up. 'I asked him if he planned to go and he was quite adamant he wasn't. He used to ring his father quite often, but somehow I think he had left Belfast and that life behind him. He didn't have the need to revisit it. But I always felt that while he wasn't close to his own family, he missed being a part of one. He got on so well with my father and he liked the close bond I had with Dad and my sisters. In many ways he had replaced his family with mine.'

At the end of two weeks Jane had to return to New Zealand for work while Ernie headed back to Tasmania to sell some wine. Flying back into Christchurch three days later he decided to stay put for a couple of days to allow him to do some business on the Monday, before heading home. Around 8 p.m. he started heading for Blenheim. He was still on the motorway on the outskirts of Christchurch when the head-on crash occurred. Ernie's Range Rover was totally destroyed, with the chassis forced back into the cab and wreckage littering the road for hundreds of metres. The truck he had hit suffered slight damage, the driver walking away with minor injuries. It took a number of hours before police arrived at Jane's door. As well as giving her the devastating news, they also needed to confirm that Ernie would have been travelling alone. 'They kept asking me over and over, if there could have been anyone else in the car with Ernie. I know they had to know, but they just kept going on about it.'

She finally asked one of the officers to ring Bill and Barbara Walsh, who were quickly on the scene. 'Jane was absolutely devastated. She didn't want to be alone but she also didn't want to talk. I thought she needed to get some rest, but she obviously couldn't sleep. In the end I brought the mattress out into the lounge and lay down with her,' Barbara says.

Ernie's death created shockwaves throughout the small community. The local radio station broadcast the news at 11.30 the next morning, while the newspaper featured the story on its front page. There were very few people who hadn't either met or known of Ernie, and all felt the loss of someone so young and full of energy.

A funeral is not the ideal situation to be meeting your in-laws for the first time. Having to phone Ernie's dad with the news of his death was hard enough for Jane, but then she had to steel herself for the initial encounter. It must have been equally as difficult for Bill Hunter, who had only ever spoken with Jane on the phone. Having lost his son, he was faced with having to provide support for a daughter-in-law he had never met. The trip out from Ireland had taken days for Ernie's family, which must have added to the torment of the occasion. It was certainly difficult for Jane trying to liaise with her own family, who were spread from Australia to Rome, Ernie's family in Ireland, and his many friends spread throughout the world. Jane was adamant Ernie shouldn't be idolised at the funeral and asked good friend Terry Dunleavy, the CEO of the New Zealand Wine Institute, to deliver the eulogy, which she herself had written. While she stood beside Terry, she was incapable of speaking about her husband in person. Walking forward to the pulpit of the church she cut a diminutive figure. The stress of the past week and the lack of sleep were etched on her face and in her bearing. As Terry talked about Ernie's many attributes and his love of everything to do with the Marlborough wine industry, Jane concentrated on her hands in what she now describes as a state of shock. The poignancy of her standing there has remained with many of the funeral-goers that day. Despite that, her inner strength was obvious to all present. Everyone who knows Jane well speaks of her steely determination and mental toughness.

It can be hard to know just what she is thinking, as she tends to internalise her emotions. Presenting a calm and composed facade she hides her inner turmoil. Her mother, Lynne, says she was impressed with the way her daughter handled herself during the torment of the funeral. 'I was surprised at some of the behaviour and how Jane was able to remain calm and composed when among other people, while she was grieving so deeply in private.'

In the build-up to the funeral the one subject that had not been broached was the future of Hunter's. Everyone knew that the company was based on Ernie's talent in marketing and promotion. Terry Dunleavy said at the time: 'Ernie had Irish charm and humour and a vital entrepreneurial spirit and keen intelligence. Whatever he tackled he did with complete commitment and dedication, underscored by common sense. He came to the wine industry when it was in general lacking a little confidence and searching for a sense of final direction, especially in relation to the exporting of New Zealand wine. Within a short time, not only was he producing wines of a startling high quality, but he showed a new style and flair in the way he marketed his wine at home and abroad. He became a hero among many of the boutique winemakers and he showed them it could be done in markets overseas, first in Australia, then in Britain and more recently on the east coast of the United States.'

Tony Laithwaite from the Sunday Times Wine Club wrote the following about Ernie:

'Someone who created such a glittering reputation for a wine estate in only five years was unlikely to be a quiet, self-effacing sort of fellow. Yet oddly enough, that's just how Ernie came across. Of course he marketed in true American style, very hard, no hesitation in letting the whole world know about every award won. Yet in conversation he always managed to imply that it was just you and him, and mostly you at that. He had an odd way of introducing your first name into every other sentence, a technique I suppose. But with the big boyish grin, the rumpled morning-after style and the Belfast accent that never faded, who minded?'

New Zealand's wine industry had lost a valuable asset, Marlborough its greatest stalwart and Jane her husband and mentor. What made his death even more tragic was the fact that Hunter's was just beginning to climb out of the depths of financial difficulty. Due to his energy and enthusiasm, Ernie had managed to place Marlborough on the world's wine map. He was just beginning to reap the benefits of all his hard work. What the future held for the up-and-coming wine company, no one knew.

Chapter 8

Upfront

A term used to describe the
appealing flavours of a wine

Everyone who loses a loved one deals with their grief in a different way. Some people rail against the world, their anger a palpable thing that controls their every move. Others pull the covers up and hide from the world, withdrawing inside themselves. There are some who throw themselves into situations in an effort to forget what has happened. It's hard to say which category Jane fell into during those early days after Ernie's death. She sought solace in the vineyards, walking for miles every day with Commodore. She cried constantly, but always in private or with very close friends. She established an impenetrable wall around her feelings in an effort to guard herself against her overwhelming grief. With Ernie gone the other mainstay of her life, her work, was placed on hold. Initially she took a six-week break from Montana as she fought to get her emotions in order. Understandably, what was going on around her held no appeal.

Taking time off work didn't even come close to providing a salve for her grief. Every night she would return to the house she had shared with Ernie. Every day she walked among the vines that were the lifeblood of his business. And throughout it all she had to make decisions that no thirty-three-year-old woman is ever prepared for. 'I was walking in a fog for weeks. Besides the pain of his death there were issues about the company that had to be resolved and I was the only one who could do that.'

As Jane tried to find her feet, questions were being raised by the industry about what would happen to Ernie's legacy — Hunter's. The company had been founded on his inimitable personality. To everyone who had dealt with him, Ernie was Hunter's Wines.

The issue of Ernie's will further complicated things, both for Jane personally and for her lawyer. David Dew says DFC had insisted Ernie write one before they acquired shares in the company in 1985. No one likes to think about death and for someone like Ernie, who lived life at breakneck speed, the necessity for a will was viewed as a hindrance, not something he seriously contemplated. Hence the rather simplistic bequeaths. Jane was left a life interest in the winery and a house in Christchurch, which had already been sold prior to Ernie's death. The rest was left to his parents and his sister's two daughters.

'Ernie had what I call a suspicious Irish nature about these sorts of things,' David Dew says. 'What that meant was he looked after his family very well.'

It was this bequeath to his parents and nieces that the man from Public Trust was referring to when he cornered Jane at Ernie's wake, saying a meeting was necessary to sort out the ownership of Hunter's. 'It was a bizarre will in that he left things to me in trust, and in the situation we didn't have children of our own, then it was to go to his nieces,' says Jane. 'It wasn't the will of anyone owning a business, it was a private will not allowing for the company he had worked hard to create. It was enough of a reason for me to want to just get out of the whole business, but I wasn't prepared to do that. We hadn't gone through all that angst for someone else who had done nothing to come along and take it away. Then again, I had excellent prospects at Montana and a career strategy planned out that didn't include giving away all I had achieved there.'

But there were a number of other factors of which she was conscious: the staff working at Hunter's at the time, the success Ernie had tasted just prior to his death, the work he had put in to create that success and the reality that the company wasn't actually worth much. While the shares had been bought back from DFC just two weeks prior to Ernie's death, Hunter's still didn't own any vineyards and had leased out the restaurant. 'It wasn't really in a state to sell. Besides, people were dependent on the winery for their livelihood and deep down I often wondered whether if Ernie hadn't been so tired and stressed from his efforts at promoting the winery, he may not have had the accident. I guess I felt I owed it to him, to at least try to carry on.'

When Tony Jordan arrived at her home one night with an expensive bottle of Australian red wine, Jane was sure he was coming to hand in his notice. 'Why would he want to stay on with me running the business? I didn't know anything about it.' Instead, Tony suggested they have something to eat and chat about the possibilities.

'I was consulting about thirty wineries at the time and I knew a fair bit about what was a good winery and what wasn't. Hunter's was a very good small winery and was starting to make some good product. It wasn't a case of us sitting down and thinking, "This is dreadful, can we make it?" We never went through that at all. I remember saying to Jane that this business had more potential than any other small winery I was consulting. I could see the opportunity for export and the opportunity for good expansion.'

Tony asked Jane what her initial thoughts were. 'I guess deep down I wanted to give it a go. I felt so strongly about what Ernie had achieved and equally as strongly about not wanting the company to be sold up — not that

I knew what I was letting myself in for back then.'

Tony suggested that if she took on the managing director's role, then he should be made a director which would give him more leverage than just being a consultant. Jane says she was surprised at his offer of commitment, especially given he was putting his backing behind a person who had never sold a bottle of wine in her life. Tony has remained a director of Hunter's ever since.

'When I look back on those days, if it hadn't been for Tony I wouldn't be here now. He was my sounding board and later he was the sounding board for the entire management team at different times. As we have matured into our own individual roles we haven't had to rely on him as much, but back in the late eighties and nineties when everything was changing he was very important. And he always made himself available. We knew that if we phoned him, he would be there for us, regardless of the fact that he was travelling all over the world with his own job. He never failed to take our calls and listen to our issues. He not only supported me but he also gave me confidence.'

Becoming managing director of Hunter's wasn't just a case of Jane continuing with her viticultural input or managing the office. She suddenly had to become the face of Hunter's, replacing Ernie. Tony told her that it was no use having the best wine in the world if no one knew about it. He knew from his experience working with Domaine Chandon in Australia that someone has to take the wine to the marketplace and get people to believe in it. 'That's why in my mind Jane had no choice. Ernie, of course, never went out as a wine expert, he went as a proprietor, whereas Jane could take a different role, coming from a technical background. Even though she has always said, "Oh, I really can't talk wine", because of her expert knowledge in viticulture and growing the grapes that make very good wine, she could go out and represent the wines as a technical and a proprietorial person. She was the obvious choice to undertake the marketing.'

When Tony told her she had to get out and start selling herself as Ernie's successor, she almost changed her mind about continuing with the business. Even today Jane finds it hard to put into words just how difficult that decision was. She had never harboured a secret desire to be a focal point for anything, let alone an emerging wine company. She hated the thought of having to talk publicly, which made her the complete opposite to Ernie. Where he loved being in the public eye, Jane revelled in being out among the vines. 'On all Ernie's trips overseas to sell, I had never travelled with him. Not just because I was working at Montana, but because I hated flying. And then Tony said to me, "If you are serious about this, then you are going to have to get yourself overseas and you have to meet everyone who is distributing Hunter's wines. You have to decide if you can work with them, and if you can't you have to let them go and find someone else." So in October I boarded a plane and over the next ten days I went round the world. This is someone who was stressed by flying and had never sold a bottle of wine in her life. I went to Italy first to see Mum and stepfather Brian, then to London, Belfast to see Ernie's parents, back to London, New York and then back home.'

Flying wasn't the only concern Jane had about her trip overseas. She was also anxious about having to make small talk with complete strangers. She is innately shy and the thought of having to hold a conversation with someone she had never met was enough to set off a migraine. 'I don't think I can explain how hard that was for me. I have got much better now but in those early years I would get myself into such a state that I would end up sick.'

One of the people she met on that initial trip was Margaret Harvey MW of Fine Wines of New Zealand, based in London. Margaret had helped pour wines for Ernie at the first Sunday Times Vintage Festival back in 1986 and now had her own distribution company, dealing with New Zealand wines only. While Hunter's was not one of her clients, she felt a bond with the emerging Marlborough-based winery. 'I got this phone call from a friend who said Jane Hunter is here and would like to meet you. So I popped down to see her, had some lunch and since then we have stayed in touch. I remember thinking at the time that there was all this talk that she would sell up the company and move back to Australia. People were saying she was a gifted viticulturist, but she wouldn't have the ability to run the business. When I met her, I thought exactly the opposite. I thought, here is a person who has no intention of selling up. I believed she would take the business on and move it forward and that she had every intention of keeping Ernie's legacy going. To me she seemed very focused.'

Initially that focus was on establishing distributors. Tony had explained how important a role this part of the wine sales chain was to the success of the company. He knew Hunter's already had some distribution networks in place, established by Ernie, but what he pointed out to Jane was she had to feel comfortable with these individuals if she wanted to grow the all-important UK and USA markets. 'Tony had advised me that I was the only one who could tell if I was able to work with someone and it was important to move on from those I didn't relate to. I quickly discovered that in a small business the distributors play an integral part. They actually become part of the business. If you remain just a client, then it is never going to work.'

While the travelling was tough, meeting old friends of Ernie was even harder. 'Meeting people like Tony Laithwaite and David Thomas who all adored Ernie was really hard. Meeting them was extremely upsetting and I had to try so hard not to break down with them. I decided that I had to take on the attitude of "Get over it, get past it", in order to survive.'

While Jane had always been a private person, it's fair to say Ernie's death accentuated that. On those early trips overseas, where she had to meet people who knew Hunter's only through Ernie, she constantly had to keep her emotions in check. While others around her could cry, Jane didn't want to break down in case they thought of her as emotionally unstable to work with. It didn't prevent her from returning to her hotel room and crying herself to sleep every night, though. Then she would get up the next day, put on a stoic face and head off to meet more business associates.

The worst experience of the visit was left until the end, when Jane went to leave New York. The decision to cancel the distributor Ernie had chosen didn't go down too well with the person involved. The resulting argument meant Jane arrived at the airport stressed out and exhausted. The only thing holding her together, she says, was the fact that she had a first-class ticket to fly to Los Angeles on an American airline, so she could relax and sleep. 'I got my ticket and my case had gone through, yet when I went to get on the flight they took my boarding pass and gave me another one for a seat in economy. Apparently Harrison Ford and Whitney Houston had arrived at the last moment and they had to remove two people from first class to accommodate them. I was one of the people who got bumped. I was furious. I was so tired and stressed and I had thought I would get on this flight and sleep for five hours. The hostess said, "It's all right, we will bring you back the first-class food." I didn't want the food and I tried to explain that to them but they wouldn't listen. By the time I got to LA I was so angry, I went straight up to the counter at the airport and told them they had to take my bags off the flight and book me a seat on the first Air New Zealand flight out of LA, in business class. And I told them they had to organise somewhere for me to stay for all the trouble they had put me through. They weren't going to do it, but I think I was so furious they realised it was better to back down.'

For those who knew her, Jane's decision to take on the Hunter's management role was no great surprise. Her mother Lynne said having experience within the wine industry since she was a child stood her in good stead. 'I think her practical experience of all aspects of wine, growing the grapes, the difficulties of growers and their relationship with wineries, vineyard management and all its problems and having an excellent sense of business were all important. And not being dazzled by the glamour of the wine business is important, probably more important than all the rest.'

Her father Brian agrees. 'I wasn't surprised when she took it on because she wouldn't be beaten.'

Her lawyer David Dew says when Ernie died the

company was in a far better financial position than it had been two or three years previously. Jane had the ability to take that further due to her many attributes. 'I always thought she could do it. She has what I call mental toughness. Her upbringing and background gave her the basis for being able to cope with running the business. In a sense you always knew she would do that better than Ernie, because she would be a better manager. He was a good marketer and promotions guy but people like that are not necessarily good at execution. Whereas I think Jane is much better at the fine detail and execution as well as better at the human relations side of the business.'

He is not the only one to look at Hunter's today and ask the question, 'Would it be as successful as it is, if Ernie had survived?' Jane might never have sold a bottle of wine in her life, or sought out distributors or even hosted tastings, but she did bring to the managing director's role a steel-trap mind and an attitude that great wine was made in the vineyards. She wasn't confrontational, although she admits she was pretty emotional at times, and she had an ability to ask for assistance when she required it. With support from the likes of Tony she was able to look at Hunter's from an entirely different perspective from that of her late husband. Wine was the core business, good wine came from quality grapes and she knew how to achieve that; all she had to do was learn how to get that end product out into the marketplace as profitably as she could.

Perhaps the greatest confirmation that she had made the right decision came from her immediate boss at Montana, Peter Hubscher. In a letter he wrote to her shortly after she resigned, he told her she had made a major impact on the company's vineyards in her three years as chief viticulturist.

'Jane, few people can ever expect to accomplish so much in such a short time. That you did it with a smile and made it work, despite the people pressures which surfaced from time to time, is a great credit to you and something you should always look back on with pride. Notwithstanding that for choice you would rather not be a managing director, I feel sure you will do a great job. Life is full of unexpected challenges. You succeeded so well with the last one that I feel confident you will quickly master the new hurdle.'

With the distributors overseas in place, the next hurdle for Jane was accepting her role as the face of Hunter's. In 1987 the winery handled just over 100 tonnes of fruit and more than half of that was being sold on the domestic market. Bill Floyd of Floyd Marketing in Blenheim could see the potential of the company and believed Jane was the perfect front person. He'd known Ernie pretty well in the preceding years, not that the two of them had always seen eye to eye. Bill describes Ernie as a 'fiery bastard', who he'd clashed with quite publicly over the Wine Festival. 'But I had a huge respect for his drive and passion and I knew the company had been predicated on his personality. It was all part of the brand. But take Ernie away from the brand and what were you left with? I thought it would be great to develop the company around Jane's own special personality.'

Jane wasn't falling over herself to follow Bill's ideas. Embarrassed that the ensuing publicity would be viewed as overt and tacky, she was struggling with letting his plan to use her for marketing go ahead. She would look him straight in the eye and challenge him to find someone else to be the focus point. As she had repeatedly said to Tony, 'What do I know about wine?'

'I always thought that Jane was such an opposite to Ernie, in a positive way,' Bill says. 'Basically they were yin and yang. But she was part of them as a couple, not just his wife, but also one of the top viticulturists in the country. It's not as though she was someone stepping out of the kitchen to take over Hunter's. She was, in fact, stepping out of the vineyard to take over.'

Bill's marketing contacts soon began to play into the company's hands. He was already working for Marlborough Cheese, who had picked up awards for their specialist products. Every time there was an event promoting the cheeses he would carefully tie it in with wine, inevitably utilising the restaurant at Hunter's. Any visiting chef would be offered the Hunter's restaurant to cook up a storm, and the visiting media were all treated to culinary delights savoured with a glass of Hunter's wine. Despite her own misgivings about promotion, Jane was the perfect ambassador for the company. Her girl-next-door good looks, her ever-present smile and her slightly nervous laugh made her the perfect subject for interviews. Bill says during those early years the media interest in her story was insatiable. 'They had a real thirst for the Jane Hunter story, because there was the tragedy of Ernie's death and the rise of her as a winery owner. You have to remember there were very few women in high-ranking positions back then. And there was something else, which is often overlooked and that's the fact she is an Australian who came over here to become a New Zealand success story.'

Something Jane was determined to do back then, and still is today, was to ensure that all the important players at Hunter's were receiving credit for what they were doing. At every opportunity she threw Tony's name to the rapacious media, and she did the same with winemaker John Belsham. She acknowledged that she couldn't have stayed on to run the company without these two men. She described Tony as the man who 'jolts us into action when we are sitting back resting on our laurels'. John, she said, 'had taken on much more of the overall company workload as well as the winemaking and had been a tower of strength.' Some of the first advertisements to appear after Ernie's death captured Jane and John holding a fistful of medals as she began integrating the staff into the overall image of Hunter's.

Yet there were still some within the industry who didn't believe Jane had the knowledge to continue Ernie's success. Brian Arnold remembers being at a function and overhearing a conversation between two Marlborough grape growers. 'They were making sarcastic comments about what did a woman think she was doing trying to run a winery and vineyard? I was standing right behind them and they had no idea who I was. I wanted to say something at the time, but I just left it. What none of them realised was Jane was putting Hunter's on a financial footing and that she had more experience than they did.'

Rural New Zealand in the mid-1980s was still very much a male-dominated environment. It was men who bought and sold the land, ran and operated the vineyards and headed all the major wine companies. That's not to say women weren't playing a vital role in any of those fields, it's just no woman had yet taken on a top position in the wine industry. That Jane had been the first female viticulturist to be employed by Montana was lost on some rather blinkered individuals. They and others who gossiped about the future of Hunter's had not taken into account Jane's pedigree, credentials or her innate ability. It was this prejudice Bill wanted to break through, in an effort to establish Jane as the focus of Hunter's. He began thinking up novel ways of getting her and the company's name into the public eye. To get national publicity, he knew he would have to gain television coverage and he knew just how to achieve that.

New Zealanders have always had a fascination for television game shows and *Sale of the Century* was no exception. Contestants had to answer a range of questions, winning money for each correct answer. At timely intervals they were then able to spend that money on items that had been donated. Screening nightly at 7 p.m. on TV One, it rocketed hosts Steve Parr and Jude Dodson to almost royalty status throughout the country, with thousands tuning in to watch the show each night. Bill could see the potential for any company whose products were included in the prize line-up. When Steve and Jude arrived in Marlborough for a promotional tour, he convinced them they should have a Hunter's Wine Village package, including a paid trip to dine at the restaurant in Marlborough and a selection of Hunter's wines. The cost of the prize was a mere pittance compared with the prime-time national coverage the company gained.

It was also important for Jane to become involved in fields outside the wine industry, she was told by both Bill and Tony. So when a position came up on the Marlborough Regional Development Board, Jane's name was put forward. Part of a government scheme to promote business innovation, the board was responsible for assessing those who had applied, to determine if a financial grant was warranted. Bill says he encouraged Jane for two reasons. 'It was another publicity paradigm, but most importantly she had something to contribute. She had a degree in horticulture, she was running a business, and she had good instincts about what could and couldn't work.'

The position also gave Jane a chance to know what was happening in the Marlborough region, besides grape growing. One company was applying to develop wasabi, another wanted to grow chestnut trees commercially, while someone else wanted to develop a koura (fresh-water crayfish) farm. It thrust her into the business world of the region and also provided her with the chance to fine-tune her own business skills, something she knew she had to do.

While Jane may have been facing up to the issues of the workplace, she couldn't deal with overseeing the renovation of the cob cottage she and Ernie had bought together just prior to his death. 'There was so much else going on that it was the last thing I really needed. I just left the builders to it. They did everything, including hanging all the pictures. When I moved in I felt like it was just a brand new home — it wasn't something that I was a part of. That came a lot later as I stamped my own mark on the property. In many ways I now regret not being more involved.'

It took some years before Jane felt at home in the renovated cottage. Initially all the walls were painted white, the garden was fairly basic and originally it was a place to retire to at the end of a day or after a trip away. As time passed, though, she began extending the house itself, adding a separate cottage for visitors, revamping the gardens, adding a swimming pool — much to the delight of her two nephews as they grew up — and placing her own mark on the historic home. While it wasn't a sanctuary to begin with, it certainly became one.

Chapter 9

Blind tasting

Tasting and evaluating a wine
without knowing what it is

Jane's first overseas marketing experience highlighted an issue that would go on to plague her for years to come — the effect arduous travel would have on her well-being. She was often ill while overseas and whereas arriving home to New Zealand was a relief, it was often followed by a period of utter exhaustion. She wasn't keen on flying and meeting strangers, and having to make small talk with them was always stressful. 'After every long-haul trip I used to end up getting very ill, which was probably due to the stress as I am not a naturally outgoing sort of person. I'm also not a very energetic person, in fact I always seem to be tired. I tell people it's because I was born two months early and am now making up for it. It's got much better but back then it was hell; it was all I could do to get through the day sometimes. I know people look at the travel and think how lucky I am but seriously it is hard work and in those early years it was all-consuming. I could never have coped with having children or anyone else in my life during that time, I didn't have the energy.'

It must have seemed that she had only just arrived home from the UK in 1987 when she was back on a plane heading there for another visit — the 1988 Sunday Times Vintage Festival. Hunter's had made history with Ernie winning the Best Dry White Wine trophy two years in a row and it was essential Jane make an appearance as the new face of the company. She entered three wines in the competition: Sauvignon Blanc, Chardonnay and Fumé Blanc. While her first overseas trip had been torturous, this one was promising to be even worse. It was like being thrown in the deep end, with Hunter's wines being compared with hundreds of other wines from all over the world. Instead of being a boost to Jane's confidence, the wins of the previous two years were a reminder that there was an expectation from the Wine Club members. Ensuring she had as much moral support as possible, her mother and stepfather arrived from Italy to assist on the Hunter's stand, as did Ernie's parents from Belfast and friends Steve and Charlotte Cohen, who were actually living in the UK. From the moment the doors opened, Club members began making their way to the Hunter's stand to try the latest offerings from Marlborough, New Zealand. There were one or two who expressed disappointment — but not in the wine, though. 'People kept coming up and saying, "The man who was here last year had oysters. Do you have any?" Of course I hadn't thought of that and there were a number of people who expressed their frustration. But we still got them to taste the wines.'

In total there were 2000 wines entered in the competition, from seventy different companies. Again the wines were judged by a panel of experts prior to the Club members making their choice on their personal favourite. It takes a lot of confidence to stand in front of a group of strangers and extol the virtues of a product that has your name on the label, and confidence wasn't something that Jane had in abundance. But Steve more than made up for her deficiency. 'Steve was a bit of an Arthur Daley-type character and he was working so hard to get people to taste the wines. At one stage he said to me, "We've split the vote on the first round, between the Fumé Blanc and the Chardonnay. What we need to do is get people to vote for just one of the wines and not both of them." So whenever someone came up to taste a Chardonnay, he would say, "No, no, you must taste the Fumé." They would say they had already tasted the Fumé and now they wanted the Chardonnay and Steve kept pouring the Fumé into their glass.'

It worked, as the Fumé Blanc 1987 was judged the best white wine at each of the three tasting sessions. In one particular tasting the public voted not only the Fumé Blanc as their favourite wine, but they also voted Hunter's Chardonnay as the second best white wine of the show. For Jane it was her first taste of success and she admits it was an exhilarating experience.

Besides the official tastings there was another important role she had to carry out while in London. It involved the auctioning off of a case of Hunter's wine that had accompanied a solo round-the-world yachtsman for well over twelve months. James Hatfield had left England in 1984, on board his 24 ft yacht *British Heart*. His aim was to raise funds for heart research, an area very close to him personally as he had spent months in hospital with a heart defect and had undergone two heart and six chest operations. Looking back on that episode of his life, James says there was an underlying motivation. 'I wanted to know if I had survived everything I had been through simply because of medical intervention, or whether there was a greater reason for me to be alive.'

During his epic trip he had called into Picton, twenty minutes from Blenheim, and gained substantial media coverage in the local paper. Taken with the story of his solo endeavour and his efforts to raise funds, Ernie had invited him for a meal at Hunter's restaurant. Enamoured by his cause and courage, he offered James a case of Hunter's wines to take back to England where it could be auctioned off at a later date. He told James he would personally run the auction at the next Sunday Times Wine Club event, if James was back by that stage. It wasn't until James arrived back in England that he was told of Ernie's death. Jane was quick to assure him that the auction would still go ahead, with her as the company representative, not her late husband. 'I felt an enormous obligation to be there for James, given how much he had been through during his trip. It was probably a far greater motivator for me to be in London than the Sunday Times Vintage Festival, if I am honest.'

Meeting James, though, was an emotional experience. 'He actually looked like Ernie, it was amazing. He was English, of course, not Irish, but he had the same sort of personality as Ernie, a bit of a rogue with a twinkle in his eye. And the fact that he had taken three years to complete his trip, had gone through three yachts, endured a sinking, serious dysentery and major storms, really impressed me. I was also impressed that he hadn't been tempted to open the wine while still at sea.'

Neither James nor Jane could have wished for a better build-up to the auction. Hunter's had just been voted as the favoured white wine of the show and when word spread that there was to be an auction of a dozen bottles, hundreds of club members descended on the small Hunter's stand where the auction was to take place. Bidding was fast and furious, with the wine selling in the end for £230, the equivalent of around NZ$56 a bottle. The relationship that began over dinner back in Blenheim in 1986 has continued to this day. James has gone on to be a major force in yachting circles in the UK. He received an MBE, was the subject of a *This is Your Life* programme and was awarded Yachtsman of the Year some ten years after his initial foray into round-the-world sailing. He and Jane kept in contact sporadically over the years and in 1997 the pair met again due to a major yachting event. Jane was in a small bookshop in Picton when she came across a book about the upcoming BT Challenge, a yacht race that begins in England and sails around the world against prevailing winds, utilising amateur crews. Thinking her father would enjoy reading about it, she flipped through the pages while waiting to be served and noticed a photo of James. With her interest raised she read on to discover that the crews taking part in the challenge were currently in Wellington, one of their round-the-world stopovers. Within an hour she had tracked James down and invited him and his crew to Blenheim for a wine tasting and a chance to raise some extra funds. The name of James' boat was *Time and Tide* and his crew of thirteen were not only amateur sailors, but they all suffered some form of disability, ranging from deafness to cerebral palsy or amputated limbs. With the motto of the yacht being 'Racing the latitudes to change attitudes', *Time and Tide* was creating a great deal of media interest. Jane decided to repeat the promotion she and Ernie had undertaken a decade earlier and gave James two cases of Hunter's wines to take home to England to auction. The crew personally signed each of the bottles before carefully stacking them safely on board. The fact the wine was going to be sailed back to England was a major drawcard for those who would later attend the auction. James himself was keen to get his hands on one of the cases.

'I underestimated how popular the wine would be and how much it would go for. I thought I should be able to afford a case, but in the end I never even got a look-in. One case went to this man from London and I approached him afterwards, explained who I was and how I would really appreciate it if I could buy just one bottle from him as a reminder of the trip and the crew who had sailed with me. He wouldn't even let me buy one bottle. He said there was no way he was going to part with any of them. "This wine is very good wine and it has created history by being sailed back here. I'm not going to sell any of it." I was stunned.'

The case of wine sold for £600, approximately NZ$1700, or $140 a bottle. All the money went to the Time and Tide Trust, along with another 5 per cent of the proceeds from Hunter's mail orders during the month following the yacht's stopover in New Zealand.

Jane's relationship with James is one of many that has endured great distances and periods of no communication.

While crowds may be anathema to her, she is very good at one-on-one situations. She has a close circle of friends whom she goes out of her way to spend time with or look out for. Many have benefited from her generosity, whether that has been shown in terms of time spent with them or events organised and paid for. Her confidence in a personal situation, though, wasn't making it any easier for her to deal with the transition from viticulturist to winery managing director. She was constantly telling anyone who would listen that she wasn't Ernie. 'The whole concept of hard sell is completely alien to the person I am and it was what he'd done so brilliantly.'

Yet those surrounding her felt differently. Tony Jordan says when Jane talked to wine buyers, she had them eating out of her hand. 'She will feign dislike of wine promotion and travel and everything else. But cut the cackle and what you find is someone who is very effective at it! The trade loves to meet her, the consumers love to meet her and when she goes out and does that sort of promotion we get sales. What's more, they aren't just flash in the pan sales but development sales in the market.'

Tony once told Jane she was like a wind-up doll. She'd arrive at a function moaning and groaning, then just before she had to meet the people it was as though someone had turned the key in her back. She would go and charm everyone around her, pausing for breath only when they had all left.

Even her father says Jane demeans herself by saying she isn't good at the marketing side of the business. 'I have been with her on a couple of marketing trips overseas and have seen it first hand. As a father it is pretty exciting to see her address a group of extremely well-off Englishmen who think they know all about wine, and to keep them spellbound. She was easily able to do that.'

While originally all her wine sales in the UK were via the Sunday Times Wine Club mail order, Jane knew she had to establish a second-tier distribution network. In Belfast she made contact with the McAlindon family, who have played an important role in the Hunter's story for the last twenty years. In Southern Ireland, distribution was taken on by Gilbey's, who are still involved at the time of writing. In Scotland, Sarah Morphew Stephen became Hunter's distributor, while Horseshoe Wines, consisting of four men, Peter Hofman, Kenneth Christie MW, David Sommerfelt and his son Neil Sommerfelt MW, became the English distributors. Over the years these people have come and gone from different distributors but all have ended up selling Hunter's wines on more than one occasion. Some, including Neil Sommerfelt MW, who is working for Hunter's current distributor Layton's, are still actively involved with the Marlborough winery.

In an era where change is the only constant, Hunter's has retained a loyal relationship with all its distributors and agents, which is one of the reasons the UK was and still is Hunter's most important market. Jane says 29 per cent of all exports go to the UK and despite the influx of Marlborough Sauvignon Blanc from other companies Hunter's has never lost its dominance in niche markets. 'Many other companies will change distributors on a regular basis, either because they feel they are not getting the best deal, or the distributor decides they want to promote a newer wine label. I'm not saying what we have is perfect and it doesn't always go swimmingly well. We have had our ups and downs but we have been and still are there for the long haul. With people like Gilbeys and the McAlindons, it's kind of like dealing with friends because our relationship goes back years. We know each other and what's more we trust each other. If anything is going to save us if the big crunch comes, I think it will be that we have developed and maintained such strong relationships within our markets. What we have is very rare and it is a very big part of the Hunter's story and our success. I know a lot of companies have dived off to other countries and while they would still say the UK and to a lesser degree Ireland is important, to us they are more than important. In a sense, they are kind of our whole being.'

Despite the inevitable influx of New World wines into the UK, Hunter's has been able to retain a niche market for more than twenty years, a market where there is less pressure on discounting or margin cutting.

While the accolades were flowing for Jane's wines at

the Sunday Times Wine Club, New Zealand as a whole was still an unknown quantity as a wine-producing region, especially in the UK. That was about to change in 1988. Two years earlier Bryan Mogridge from Montana had discovered first hand the importance of having a presence at an overseas event. Montana wines were being shown for the first time at the influential London Wine Trade Fair in London, on the Seagrams stand. (Seagrams had a shareholding in Montana at the time.) This particular trade fair was renowned for singling out a country as host for the event. Having that honour allowed the country to fete media and buyers, through luncheons, dinners and guest speakers. In 1986, the host country was Australia and Terry Dunleavy says the impact that fair had on Bryan was very strong. 'He was also the chair of the New Zealand Wine Institute and he came back to New Zealand saying, "We have to be there." Apparently, the Australians had told Bryan they would double their UK wine sales as a result of being the host nation. He asked me to try to get the organisers to accept New Zealand as a host nation for 1987. That was a huge ask. We had never even been to the Trade Fair as a nation, so it was a bit much to expect them to offer us the hosting rights first up.'

Terry was right — the organisers weren't prepared to provide hosting rights to a country that had never taken part. So in 1987 for the first time, New Zealand wine made an appearance at the London Wine Trade Fair and created a major stir. The impact was so strong the organisers agreed to give New Zealand the hosting rights for 1988. Even though Hunter's wine was all pre-sold, Jane knew that it was vital the company be represented at such a major event, even if it did mean she yet again had to pack her bags and travel halfway round the world. As hosts, the dozen New Zealand wine companies taking part had a central third-floor stand and were able to promote their wines and local produce at an invitation-only formal luncheon. The meal, featuring New Zealand produce, was prepared by ex-New Zealand chef Glynn Christian, who was renowned in London at the time. With stunning weather on the day, guests were treated to aperitifs including Hunter's Sauvignon Blanc, prior to the gourmet luncheon. This was no staid English affair. Instead, the luncheon was set in a garden on the sixth floor of the Kensington Exhibition building. A creek flowed along the edge of the perfectly manicured lawns, with ducks and flamingos gracing the waterway. Jane thought the flamingo statues were a little over the top, especially for a London scene, until she noticed them tuck their heads under their wings.

Pink stucco buildings highlighted by jasmine-adorned architraves made the entire venue almost surreal, especially once you remembered you were sitting six floors above London. The luncheon was the first in a wide range of events for all the wine industry personnel involved. Wine writers, the London Connection (New Zealand businessmen working in the city) and a multitude of trade personnel were guests of the industry throughout the week, while the wines themselves were on show at the Fair. With Hunter's success at the recent Sunday Times Wine Festival, Jane was one of a number of industry personnel asked to present the first New Zealand Wine seminar held at the eleventh-century Vintner's Hall. As she would often do in the future, she focused on her area of expertise, the growing of grapes, rather than the production of wine. It also gave her the chance to promote Marlborough and its ability to produce cool-climate wines with distinctive flavours. It was a speech that very nearly didn't happen, as Jane succumbed to a flu virus that was doing the rounds of the Wine Fair. Once again she had become sick following the travel and on this occasion lost her voice. 'It has become the standard joke that when I arrive in England I get a call from the distributors to see whether or not I have a voice. I couldn't tell you the number of times I have got to a wine show and all I have been able to do is croak.'

London was no different. Jane, along with a number of other wine representatives, ended up having to deal with the effects of the flu while trying to promote their wines. This, combined with standing behind a stall for eight hours a day, answering the same questions about the wines over and over, meant the trip was a gruelling one. But the results made up for it. By the end of the trade fair orders were close to surpassing volume.

When Jane arrived home she brought with her expressions of interest from a large number of potential buyers. It was becoming increasingly obvious that Hunter's would need to expand beyond their current production just to meet demand. But for wine, grapes were required; and since the majority of vineyards had been sold in 1985, the company had been reliant on the small block it owned at the back of the winery and contract growers. In a serendipitous moment at the end of 1988, Jane was offered the opportunity to buy back one of the original Hunter's blocks. Russell Jackson, who had bought eight hectares alongside the winery, was keen to on-sell it. Jane, though keen to see part of the company's heritage returned, was not financially secure enough to purchase it on her own. She spoke at length about it with her father, who not only agreed that she needed to buy back the land but offered to go into partnership with her. They decided to buy the property under the auspices of a shell company, which they managed to pick up from their lawyer for just $5. The company, Mertop, bought Russell out, Jane secured the vineyard for the company and Russell Jackson offered to stay on as the vineyard manager.

Brian says the partnership with his daughter has been an amiable one, although he adds with a smile that the vineyard never seems to make any money. 'Because whenever Jane wants to try a new variety, that's where she puts it.'

The joint venture would provide another tier in an already strong relationship between father and daughter. Brian was a strong adviser as Jane contemplated development of the company. Even today when he no longer has any involvement in the Australian wine industry, he takes an active interest in his own slice of Marlborough's wine industry growth.

Chapter 10

*A term given to wine to indicate that
it is of higher quality than usual*

As a viticulturist for Montana Jane had gained some rudimentary knowledge of business, especially given her role in establishing annual grape prices with contract growers. She had also run a successful business with her cafe in Waikanae. Yet she was the first to admit that those forays into the world of company finances weren't enough to help her run a growing business. She initially sought help from her lawyer, David Dew, explaining that she needed assistance if she was to come to grips with the financial implications of taking over Hunter's. The accountant Ernie had used was based in Christchurch and the distance was impacting on her ability to make quick decisions. With David's help she employed Mark Peters, a Blenheim-based accountant, who would later go on to have a major role in the wine industry as Chairman of the Board of the New Zealand Wine Company.

'Financially at that stage, which would have been late 1988, it was all a bit of a mess,' he says. 'Understandably, everyone was rushing around trying to keep the business going and it was more important to get the wine made and sold than worry about everything else. I think Jane quickly realised that she would be better off to have one or two advisers, where she could make her own decisions rather than having a board of governance which she would have to report to.'

The board of governors was a flow-on from Ernie's convoluted will which had left Jane with a life interest in the winery. The actual running of the company was placed in the hands of trustees. One was a good friend of Ernie's, Barry Atkinson QC, who had been paramount in his many legal battles over the years; another was a friend, Suzanne Sniveley. As managing director Jane had to report to the trustees and invariably couldn't make a business decision without their approval. That scenario was problematic, given the necessity to make decisions on the spot. The board was stymieing Jane's ability to take control of the company and manage it in the best way possible. Tony Jordan had foreseen the problems early on, which was why he was adamant he be made a director of the company. 'It meant he could fight on my behalf. He was backwards and forwards from Australia like a yo-yo during this time period. All I ever needed to do was call him and he would be there for me.'

He was also a principal believer in Jane employing consultants as and when she needed them, which Jane admits was the making of the business. She would seek out suitable individuals she could work with and call on them only when they were required. Not only did it minimise the management structure but long term the financial outlay was far less and it provided flexibility for the company.

It didn't take her long to realise that answering to a board was not the most beneficial way of running the company. She convinced the trustees that it would be more advantageous if they disbanded as a board and left the company decision-making to her and Tony. While they agreed with handing the reins back to her, Jane still had to fight the issue of who actually owned Hunter's. Despite all the efforts she had put in with the overseas trips, the marketing and selling of the wine, Jane still only had a life interest in the company. The ownership issue was turning into a major battle. David Dew was one of three lawyers given the task of trying to sort out the legal ramifications. He urged Jane to file a claim under the Matrimonial Properties Act as well as a claim under the Family Protection Act, in an effort to challenge the will. During the three-year legal fight, Jane never knew whether or not she was going to lose the lot. 'For me it was a case of going through all this angst and yet not knowing whether or not I owned the place. I wasn't about to sit back and let someone else take it over. Ernie wouldn't have wanted that.'

It was that exact line the lawyers took. On the issue of when the will had been written, the judge was told the following:

'It was made while [Ernie] was under some pressure in the business and early on in his marriage. He did not foresee the future, but saw this as a temporary expedient to satisfy their [DFC's] requirements. The evidence showed that in more recent times before his death, he spoke of his intention to ensure that the plaintiff was made a partner in the business and vineyard. His solicitor speaks of fifty per cent ownership. The bank manager at the time always thought they [both] had owned it. The deceased had outstanding managerial, promotional and marketing skills, but limited knowledge of the intricacies of grape growing and winemaking. It was the plaintiff who supplied these skills and without them the business would not have prospered.'

It was pointed out that during Ernie's many trips overseas, it had been Jane who ran the company, both from the viticultural and the business points of view.

At the end of three years a ruling gave Jane total

shareholding of the company and awarded a payout to Ernie's two nieces and his father. 'That was a big call, as the payments amounted to almost a third of the value of the company at that time,' David Dew says. 'She had to turn around and raise that money to pay the family out. It was an incredibly stressful time, but at least now Jane owned the company outright.'

With her name securely on the company ownership papers Jane was finally able to take steps forward, even if initially they were only incremental steps. Alongside Mark Peters she had also hired Colin Notley, a Christchurch-based financial consultant. Renowned for his strong commercial background, he would later go on to become the president of the New Zealand Institute of Chartered Accountants. Recommended to her by business associates, he was first approached by Jane towards the end of 1988 when the company was beginning to lift itself out of financial difficulties. Although flattered by the offer, he did warn her: 'If you are reliant on my knowledge of wine, then I am going to be in trouble.' Colin brought with him solid financial expertise, although he was adamant he didn't want to be taken on as an employee. 'He has always worked on the principle that if I need him he will be there, but he never wanted to be paid a retainer; he considered that a waste of money.'

Colin says despite the fact Jane had successfully run her own business with Tootlebury's, she lacked confidence.

'The fact she asked for help should never have been seen as a sign of weakness. Even in those early days she was quite capable of understanding the issues. To think of her as a dolly bird would be an absolute travesty. She was a business lady but she had been thrown into the deep end and she needed someone to hold her hand. She never needed people to make the decisions for her, she just needed people to give advice. And she never took that advice willy nilly. She was quite capable of making her own mind up. She is very decisive, she can make a decision very quickly. She doesn't muck around.'

One of the first decisions she had to make as the new owner was whether or not to expand. Not surprisingly, Jane was cautious about growing too quickly. Given how close the company had come to folding in the mid-1980s, there was no way she wanted to rack up huge debts just because the company had experienced success in the international market. Her own conservative approach was supported by both Tony Jordan and Colin Notley. 'I suggested maybe we should be conservative in the amount of gearing we were prepared to undertake,' Tony says. 'She had concerns about the amount of debt she was prepared to carry and knew that she would have to borrow from the bank if she wanted to expand in any way. So we set a limit on that. We always knew whatever we wanted to do, we had a limit on how much borrowing we could undertake and we wouldn't be able to go above that no matter what.

It meant she wasn't going to get into any trouble, as it was easy to service.'

In hindsight, though, Tony believes they may have set that limit too low. 'I look back on it now and say if we had set twice that limit, the business could have expanded a lot more rapidly. It might have been much bigger today if we had done that but equally I was able to walk away and go back to Australia and know that the bailiffs weren't going to come knocking on her door.'

Colin says hindsight is a wonderful thing and agrees that if they had been more daring maybe Hunter's would be bigger today than it is. 'But there again, if we hadn't taken that conservative approach we may have struggled to survive. And it wasn't unreasonable that Jane was conservative, especially when you consider how tough things had been only a few years earlier.'

Jane doesn't regret her earlier conservatism, in fact she says it has helped rather than hindered Hunter's name over the years. 'I have never seen volume as being a plus. Just because you get bigger, it doesn't mean your brand is any easier to sell or you are more profitable. Instead, what often happens when you grow is that your product becomes a commodity. Size to me isn't the be-all and end-all. Yes, we could have grown, but if we had done that we probably would have had to forgo independence, shareholding and maybe integrity and quality. We have chosen to stay in what is probably the harder part of the market — the smaller part. Selling into restaurants, independent wine shops and via direct mail can be a lot harder than selling into a chain of supermarkets — but the upside is that you become known as a brand rather than as a producer of Marlborough Sauvignon Blanc, which has become somewhat of a commodity.'

However, it became blatantly obvious to everyone at Hunter's, Jane included, that the company couldn't afford to sit still in terms of development. Mark Peters says they made the decision to double throughput. 'We needed to expand the infrastructure to ensure we could handle that amount of fruit the next year. The only problem was, we didn't have double the amount of fruit coming in and given that it takes three years for plantings to come on stream, we knew it would be some years before we did. So in the interim period Jane decided to use the winery for contract winemaking.'

There has always been a sense of people helping each other in Marlborough's wine circles. The first 1985 Cloudy Bay wines were made at the Corbans winery in Gisborne, while later Corbans would use the Cloudy Bay winery to produce their Stoneleigh Wines. Yet no one was producing wines on behalf of other labels on a regular basis. It was a canny business move, not only for Hunter's but also for companies such as Delegat's, Matua Valley and Coopers Creek, which utilised the service. In previous years their fruit had been transported to their own Auckland- or

Gisborne-based wineries, adding to the cost of production. There was also the ever-present danger that the fruit could deteriorate before it reached its destination. Having a winery within Marlborough prepared to not only juice the fruit but also make the wine was a positive step forward, particularly in terms of quality. For Hunter's it meant they were able to maximise the new facilities and earn an income to help offset costs until they could source more fruit of their own.

At the end of the 1989 vintage, on 23 April, the new-look winery was officially opened. The former wine shop was moved from under the mulberry tree and incorporated into the new office building, providing Hunter's with a specialised home where wine trophies, award certificates, media write-ups and the full range of wines available could be shown off in style. That is, if you could get past Commodore, who instantly discovered a love for the front of the wine shop table. The foot traffic was a huge component of Hunter's business, especially given the fact there were very few cellar doors in Marlborough. Hunter's was still the only winery that had a restaurant on site and the media hype over the wine and Jane herself ensured a steady stream of visitors. As winemaker John Belsham says, the Hunter's story had captured the hearts of consumers. 'There was clearly this sympathy vote for the company, which had been founded by a charismatic character who had ended up being tragically killed. It was the fairy-tale story of the grieving widow taking over the business and succeeding, along with an enthusiastic winemaker and a highly qualified technical Australian consultant. You can see the picture in the buyers' mind. It was something everyone wanted to get into.'

Another lure was that Jane had been named as one of the world's five best women winemakers, which she still finds amusing these days, given she is a viticulturist and not a winemaker. 'When I used to give talks in the early days, the first thing I would do is say, "I'm not a winemaker, I'm a viticulturist so don't ask me any difficult winemaking questions. Secondly I am not a New Zealander, I am an Australian, so don't make rude comments about the Aussies."'

Columnist for the London *Saturday Express* Oz Clarke didn't seem to mind splitting hairs over her actual occupation. He nominated Jane as one of the five best women winemakers in the world, alongside luminaries such as Madame de Lencquessaing of France's Chateau Pichan Lalande Pauillac, Ros Ritchie of Delatite Winery in Australia, Marilisa Allegrini of Valpolicella Allengrini in Italy, and Madame Lalou Brize of Burgundy's Domaine dela Romani in Conti. It was heady stuff that Jane only found out about when Ernie's father sent her the newspaper clipping with the details. It wasn't an official ranking, more an end-of-the-year rundown on the most important people from the previous twelve months. But for Jane it was a confidence booster. And it was a brilliant marketing tool that was used extensively for years to come.

Jane's steady hand at the helm of Hunter's was not going unnoticed. Terry Dunleavy was the CEO of the New Zealand Wine Institute at the time and was keen to get her involved in the national machinations of the industry. During the London Wine Trade Fair in 1988 he had seen the impact she had on wine buyers and the media and believed she had an enormous amount to offer. He suggested that she put herself up as a member of the Institute. Given there were no South Island representatives or any women on the board at the time, it's understandable she was reluctant. 'I wasn't too keen, but Terry wanted me to build my confidence and get to know the industry a bit better. Marlborough was so new, yet growing so fast, that he knew it needed to be represented.'

With the impact of hosting the London Wine Trade Fair behind them, the industry was in a positive state, particularly as export orders began to filter through. Yet there were issues that had to be dealt with. Excise tax was the bane of nearly every winery owner. Jane was no different. 'New Zealand wine was spearheading a huge export drive. Whenever anyone went overseas they would serve New Zealand wine. We used to say that unlike the New Zealand food industry, the wine came to the table, sat on the table with the label which said "product of New Zealand" and was very much in everyone's face. As we have struggled to open new export markets, we could have used the money we were paying in excise tax to put into our business. It would have helped us expand. Then when Goods and Services Tax (GST) came in, we were all told it would be the only tax we had to pay. But with wine, we got stuck with GST on top of excise; in other words we had a double tax.'

Another major concern was the impact phylloxera was having in the North Island. With the industry on a roll, the replanting of major tracts of vineyard was holding back growth. Then there were the issues that are still around now, despite decades having come and gone.

'The wine industry seems to go in cycles. The New Zealand dollar was high, interest rates were high and there was an incredible amount of planting going on. As an industry we were worrying about where we were going to sell the ensuing wines and we also knew that we needed to develop new markets — that was a major issue. A bit like it is now.'

In an effort to address that one particular issue, Terry was placed in charge of establishing an export wing within the Wine Institute. All companies interested in exporting were invited to become an inaugural member of what would be known as The Export Wine Guild. Hunter's was one of the original twenty to sign up. Funded by a voluntary levy from all participating wineries, it was a unique promotional wing for the New Zealand wine industry, with all efforts initially concentrating on the UK. There was a good reason why this market was chosen above any others. A quantity of New Zealand wine was already being sold into the UK and advice back from all the inaugural winery members indicated it was their chief market, far greater than Australia or the USA. The Guild produced a tight-knit bunch of industry personnel that included Terry, Rosemari Delegat from Delegat's Wines, Bill and Ross Spence from Matua Valley, John Hancock of Morton Estate, along with the big companies of Montana and Corbans. Rosemari was the initial chair and says there was always a sense of camaraderie that other countries couldn't comprehend. 'Those days were fantastic; we worked very hard and there was a united determination to succeed. There was never any question that we wouldn't succeed, which was demonstrated time and time again by people pouring each other's wines. That surprised the wine buyers and the media. We could never understand what all the fuss was about. We had come a very long distance and were only going to be there for a very short time, so we never thought twice about helping each other. And it wasn't hard to talk about each other's wines and the regional characteristics because we knew the wines intimately. That willingness to share was unique, I think, and I don't think it exists in the industry now.'

Once Vicky Bishop was appointed as the UK Wine Guild manager, the opportunity to promote New Zealand wines gained impetus. Distributors were keen to show off the wines to agents around the country and inevitably would request a member of the Guild be present at a tasting. Jane was a popular speaker, partly because of the Hunter's story and also because she was a female viticulturist. 'I spent a huge amount of time when I was in the UK doing tastings, not just of Hunter's wines but New Zealand wines in general. Vicky would always tell me that the aim was to promote New Zealand, but she would always ensure that there were a few Hunter's wines within the tasting, so we got very good publicity. I found those early events very daunting because I always expected the audience would want to hear from a winemaker. If I knew I was going to have to conduct a tasting I would ensure I got all the wines that were being included sent to me and would go through them with winemakers John Belsham or Gary Duke and of course Tony Jordan, and listen to what they had to say about them so I could repeat that. But when I got up to speak I ended up talking about viticulture and regionality, which I understood. I would discuss issues like phylloxera, which stunned many people because European winemaking nations would never admit to something like phylloxera. In the end it seemed to appeal to people because they weren't being bombarded with technical issues like pH and acid levels. I wasn't the only New Zealander over there promoting our wines but I think I was the only female viticulturist who was.'

For someone who wasn't keen on public speaking, Jane quickly learnt how to hide her nerves — from the audience at least. 'It was only because I was getting a tremendous amount of support from the rest of the Wine Guild members that I was able to do that. Initially, everyone else was also speaking at various occasions. I would do the viticultural aspect, Terry would speak about the industry overall, while someone else would cover the winemaking. There was a huge support network. If that hadn't been there I could never have fronted up, I just wouldn't have been able to do it.'

But while she was able to mask her fear of public speaking, she wasn't quite as adept at covering up her fear of flying, according to Rosemari. 'I remember one occasion when we were leaving London on our way to New York. It was at the time that the English noise abatement laws came into effect. Typical us, we got on board and never realised that the plane was stopping off somewhere on the way to pick up more passengers. So we take off from the airport, throttle up and head through the clouds getting out of the traffic of Heathrow, which always scares the pants off Jane. Then the engines throttle back and we appear to be just gliding. Jane looked at me and I looked at her and before we knew it we were desperately clutching each other's hands. Jane was worse than me but I have to admit I was feeling a bit nervous. We were terrible flying companions really because neither of us was in the least bit comfortable so we couldn't help allay the other person's fear. Just as we were starting to panic and crush each other's hands, the pilot comes on the speaker explaining that there was no need for concern as they were just following noise abatement laws and would be picking up speed shortly as we travelled towards Manchester. That was a relief, but then we realised that he had said we were heading for Manchester and we thought we were going to New York. We were almost hysterical. Here we were, two mature businesswomen who had travelled right around the world and yet couldn't even get on the right plane to New York. We stood up and tried to attract the attention of the air hostess and noticed that Nick Nobilo from New Zealand was in a seat behind us. Again we just looked at each other because we knew Nick was heading to New York, the same as we were. Therefore we must be on the right plane. It was a case of sitting back down as quickly as possible and pretending nothing had happened. It was a flight neither of us has ever forgotten.'

There is only one thing that comes close to getting out into the marketplace and personally selling your wine to the consumer and that is getting others to do it for you via the printed word. Jane had been the subject of dozens of interviews and articles since taking over the company in 1987. There is something endearing about the story of the grieving widow taking on the world and making a success of it. This was all good news for the company,

Three little girls, Libby, Ashley and Jane Arnold — all set for church in 1960.

While working on Edward Kennedy's presidential campaign in 1980, Jane was allowed into the inner sanctum of his office in Boston.

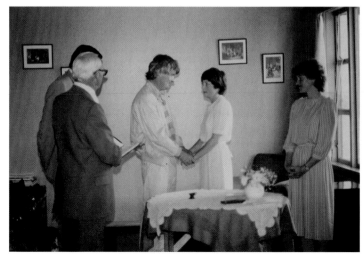

Ernie and Jane taking their vows on 4 May 1984. Bridesmaid Jo Deans is on the right.

Jane, Ernie and a rather large boating companion in the form of Commodore, at Penzance Bay.

A victorious Ernie Hunter, after he surprised the world by winning at the Sunday Times Vintage Festival in the UK, with his Marlborough Fumé Blanc. Wine writer Hugh Johnson is on his right.

Outside the original Hunter's winery: Ernie, Tony Laithwaite (from the London Sunday Times Vintage Festival) and winemaker John Belsham.

Weighing in at 95 kg, Commodore dwarfed the petite Jane.

The McAlindon family in Belfast have been distributing Hunter's wines for more than twenty years. From left: sons Neil, Peter and their father Kevin with Jane.

Winemaker Gary Duke, Jane and the award-winning 1991 Sauvignon Blanc which won, among other things, the Marquis de Goulaine Trophy for the Best Sauvignon Blanc in the World.

Jane with the love of her life for fifteen years, Paddy — a Clumber Spaniel who never missed a chance to grab the spotlight.

On one of her many tours through the UK, Jane with from left: Vicky Bishop, manager of the UK Wine Guild; Tony Coles, Heritage Wines; Julian Clutterbuck, AH Wines; David Cook of WM Steadman Ltd; and Peter Hoffman, Horseshoe Wines.

Jane donated two cases of Hunter's wines to James Hatfield MBE to help raise funds for his Time and Tide Trust. The wines were sailed back to England and auctioned, raising the equivalent of NZ$140 a bottle, with all funds going to the Trust.

Best friend Liz Moran, from Australia, has been a constant support to Jane over the years.

Jane with her father Brian Arnold and sister Libby Macdonald, shortly after receiving her OBE in 1993.

Presenting her speech to 1000 graduates, after receiving her Honorary Doctorate from Massey University.

The management team of Hunter's: Jane, Mac (Peter Macdonald) and Gary Duke — with the ever-present Paddy.

Celebrating together in Singapore, Jane with her sisters Libby and Ashley and mother Lynne.

Being presented with the inaugural Women in Wine Award at the International Wine and Spirits Competition in 2003. From left: Guiseppina Viglierchio, President of Le Donne del Vino, and Chas Dahlback, President of IWSC.

While in Vietnam in 2007, Jane made friends with the New Zealand party participating in the Wine and Food Week in Saigon.

The next generation. Jane's nephews James and Edward Macdonald.

Family is all-important to Jane and they celebrate whenever they can. Here at her father's eightieth birthday: Libby, Ashley, their father Brian and Jane.

After twenty years on her own, Jane has finally found companionship with Graeme Coates. The couple recently visited the India Cricket Club in Mumbai, during a promotional trip for Hunter's.

even if Jane winced every time she picked up a magazine and saw her face plastered over the pages. But while it was promoting her achievements, it wasn't promoting the quality of the wine. That was to change when in 1989 UK-based magazine *Decanter* gave the biggest accolade of all to Hunter's. *Decanter* plays an important role in the making and breaking of wine companies. If your wine can achieve a ninety-plus score, which is deemed a perfect example of the variety, then you are on the road to success. Prior to 1989 no New Zealand Sauvignon Blanc had been included in the regular magazine tastings. This year, though, there were two wines, one from Hunter's and the other also a Marlborough wine from Jane's former employer, Montana. The two local wines were up against 128 others from all over the world, with the largest contingent of entrants coming from France. It was a turning point for all of New Zealand when Hunter's took out the top honours. If the French had been concerned when Hunter's took the top prize in London back in 1986, there must have been considerable unease when they discovered that not only had Hunter's Sauvignon Blanc been judged by *Decanter* magazine as the best in the world but in second equal place was the other Marlborough wine, Montana's Sauvignon Blanc, which had tied for points with the Burgundian Domain du Relais de Poste 1987.

John Belsham says it was another case of surprising all the pundits. 'We couldn't put a foot wrong at this time.

Every time we put a wine into a show we would win gold medals or a trophy. It was an amazing run. But we had good fruit to start with and with Tony's experience we were starting to produce some very smart wines. When you are in that situation you are a step ahead of your competition.'

It was a fantastic boost for the Hunter's distributors in the UK. Once again the orders began to flow in as word spread of this stunning new winegrowing region down in New Zealand. But Hunter's were almost denied the right to celebrate the win at home due to the stubborn refusal by local paper the *Marlborough Express* to print the correct ranking. The first newspaper article reported that Hunter's and Montana were tied for first place. Despite numerous phone calls from Jane to the editor, the story was not changed. In the end, the editor of *Decanter* magazine, Tony Lord, personally wrote to the paper explaining the ranking system and confirming that Hunter's alone had been awarded the top honour. It was a small victory for Jane, who had been furious at the lack of local acknowledgement.

The same wine went on to win the trophy for best Sauvignon Blanc at the Air New Zealand National Wine Show later that year. But it wasn't only Sauvignon Blanc that was turning heads. Hunter's Pinot Noir 1988 was highly recommended in *Decanter* just a few weeks after the Sauvignon Blanc had been awarded the top honour.

'In hindsight it was a terrible wine, we didn't have the clones right back then, but it was a special moment for the winemakers.'

Twenty years on, Pinot Noir has become one of the strong arms of the Marlborough wine industry and the acknowledgement of the Hunter's wine in 1989 was the first step towards that.

Chapter 11

Cultivating

Breaking the soil down into fine particles, providing optimum conditions for the vine to grow

The parochialism of New Zealand is never more apparent than when a top award is bestowed on one of its own. Sporting accolades perhaps gain the most attention but achievements in other fields are equally important. It does a lot for the psyche of this small country to see a company compete against another much bigger and come out the winner. So it was with Hunter's wines. Jane finds it ironic that New Zealanders weren't prepared to rate the wines from their own country until international experts gave them the seal of approval. With accolades such as the Sunday Times Wine Club wins and the write-ups by *Decanter*, Hunter's and Marlborough wines were suddenly being rated by New Zealand consumers.

It became apparent to the wine industry overall that domestic consumption was about to increase and there was a need to ensure the wines were easily accessible to the general public.

In the late 1980s the only place you could buy wine, in fact any alcohol, was a liquor store, which is why the New Zealand Wine Institute was closely watching the Sale of Liquor Amendment Act, which would create more licences for wine and other alcoholic beverages. While the Act promised to modernise the very antiquated liquor licensing laws, it wasn't going far enough for the Wine Institute's liking. An amendment that would have allowed the sale of table wine in supermarkets and grocery stores had been tabled but this was thwarted when the Act was considered at committee level. A survey of customers at three major Auckland supermarkets showed unprecedented demand for the right to buy wine with groceries, forcing the government to rethink the amendment. Jane clearly remembers the day she heard that their wish had been granted. 'We were at a two-day conference of the Wine Institute at the Hotel du Vin, when Terry came in and told us he had just heard the news. We were so excited and we celebrated that night believing it was the best thing out for the industry. In hindsight, we should have been kicking ourselves. Supermarket sales, while they were good in the beginning, have caused some major headaches since. When we first started putting our wines into supermarkets we received the same margin as we got anywhere else. Now, though, with only two major chains, we have lost control over the margins. A lot of people in supermarket wine departments are not allowed to take samples so therefore they have no understanding of what they are selling. And the chains appear to be interested only in getting the best deal they can. They want to discount wines and use them as a loss leader to get people through the door. That is why these days so many companies concentrate on export only — the domestic market is just too damn hard. We had no idea of what was around the corner when we celebrated that Act being passed.'

On 1 April 1990, the first supermarket licences were handed out. For the first time consumers could buy their bread, eggs, meat and wine all from the one store. Within a few years, wine would be the second-most popular purchase item at supermarkets.

The move from liquor outlets to grocery stores placed additional pressure on the marketing of Hunter's wines. Jane realised she would need to increase the company's profile in a different way if she was to capture the new consumer who was buying wine with their steak. 'We realised that we would have to start marketing ourselves beyond the winery. We had never had a New Zealand distributor, as we had always had our own sales team plus cellar door, restaurant and mail order. But with the advent of supermarket sales I knew we had to place ourselves in front of the buyers and the consumers.'

Karen Rose was the sales representative for Hunter's, initially in Nelson and Marlborough and later throughout the South Island. With the belief that you can't encourage a person to buy a wine unless they have sampled it first, Jane suggested they do tastings in supermarkets. It was a great idea but one that Karen quickly realised didn't meet the approval of many other Marlborough producers. 'Hunter's was the first local winery to actually get their product into supermarkets and I think people resented it because Jane had thought of it and they hadn't. There were a number of comments from other producers along the lines of "Fancy Hunter's demeaning themselves by dump stacking their wine."' (Dump stacking is a phrase used when producers sell their wines into a mass market, such as a supermarket chain.) 'I remember many of the well-known producers saying, "That'll be the day when I dump stack." Now everyone sells in supermarkets, even those who were really reluctant to ever go down that path. It was an innovative move by Jane, but then again she has always been innovative when it comes to business.'

As more New Zealanders became aware of the wines coming out of Marlborough, the success of the annual Wine Festival grew. What had begun as a few hundred visitors had grown exponentially. In 1990, close to 17,000 individuals descended on Brancott Estate to sample the best the region had to offer. They came from all over the country, with major sponsor Air New Zealand scheduling special flights into the region specifically for the day. Marlburians became accustomed to waking up to the sound of Boeing planes flying overhead in the early hours of the morning and late in the evening as thousands of people travelled to and from Auckland, Wellington and Christchurch. (At the time Fokker Friendships and smaller commuter planes were the only aircraft servicing the area, which made the arrival of a string of Boeings so notable.) At the 1990 festival Hunter's decided to move away from promoting just wine and combined with Riverlands Meats to endorse the matching of wine with food. Each year the wineries competed against each other to see who could come up with the best decorations. This year Jane decided she needed to create a lasting impression of Hunter's. 'I remember coming into the winery on the morning of the festival and picking all these vine leaves so we could create a pergola stretching out from our tent site. It was a replica of the trellised vines that we have in front of the winery and it proved almost too successful, given how hot a day it was. The shade it provided to those standing underneath meant people trying our wines didn't want to move on.'

The decorations, combined with the food available and entertainment from the likes of the local barbershop quartet, saw Hunter's with teammates Riverlands Meats judged the best site of the festival. There were thousands of drinkers and more than one trip back to the winery for extra stocks was necessary. Despite people being able to buy just a tasting of wine and not a glassful, the company sold more than 130 cases of wine — over 1560 bottles. These days, with so many more wineries in the region the sales on festival day are miniscule in comparison. There has also been a notable change in what people are choosing to sample. 'In those early years people were drinking Breidecker because it was our cheapest wine. But at the 2008 festival the most popular choice was MiruMiru™, our sparkling wine, which was the most expensive.'

One of the strict rules of Marlborough's Wine Festival is that no company can sell bottles of wine on site. Early licensing laws also prevented cellar doors opening on the Sunday of Wine Festival weekend, so companies couldn't capitalise on the interest shown at the festival itself. However, if you had a mail-order business you were granted permission to be open to process orders for wine. Initially, Hunter's was one of the few in Marlborough to have mail order and as a consequence they were allowed to open, resulting in thousands of dollars worth of orders being placed on the Sunday.

In 1990 Marlborough got another chance to promote itself on a large scale when Queen Elizabeth II was the guest of honour at a luncheon held at Montana's Brancott Estate. The timing of the visit was four days after the massive festival, which caused some serious headaches for the Queen's security personnel. Initially they wanted the organisers to can the festival altogether, obviously concerned that some would-be terrorists could take advantage of the huge crowds and establish a hiding hole to wait out in until the Queen arrived. Montana's Gerry Gregg says the suggestion to cancel the festival was never taken seriously by organisers, which meant security officials had to find other ways of ensuring the Queen's safety. They decided to place snipers around the vineyard for the days leading into the festival and the four days after. It wasn't until years later that anyone heard about the secret gun-toting guards, which gives an indication of how well hidden the snipers were.

On the day of the Queen's visit a silk-lined marquee was erected and 450 wine-industry luminaries were invited to dine with Her Majesty. Coinciding with the 38th conference of the New Zealand Wine Institute, the visit was deemed an outstanding success. For the fledgling Marlborough wine industry it was an auspicious occasion, with many of the winemakers and company owners — including Jane and John — given the chance to personally meet Queen Elizabeth. When the Queen was photographed sipping a Montana Sauvignon Blanc, the subsequent publicity for the industry overall was a marketing dream. In fact, Jane had to leave the event early as British wine writer Jancis Robinson MW had given her a special task to carry out.

'You have to remember this was before cellphones and text messaging. Jancis had phoned me the day before the luncheon and asked if I could race back to the winery straight after the event and phone her to let her know if the Queen had actually drunk a Sauvignon Blanc in public. That's how important it was considered.'

It was supposedly the first time Her Majesty had been captured drinking wine in public. The Marlborough industry was about to make the most of the fact that it was one of their wines she sipped, with shots of the event flashed around the world in a matter of hours.

All the publicity was helping to fuel international interest in Marlborough as a region of renown. Many Australian companies in particular were keen to secure a foothold in the province. Already Marlborough was home to West Australian-based Cape Mentelle, who set up Cloudy Bay Wines and was followed by companies such as Wolf Blass and Yalumba. The faith these companies showed by purchasing land was a welcome reinforcement of the wines that had already been produced. But there were others who weren't quite as popular with the locals. A few Australian conglomerates were reputedly buying small parcels of grapes for processing in Australia, blending with their own home-grown grapes. During a Radio New Zealand interview with Maggie Barry, Jane summed up the feeling of Marlborough's wine industry. 'We've had quite a few Australian companies planting grapes and going into partnership with wineries in this area. The people who are here and show up front and put dollars in are not the problem. But I think there are a lot of growers who are selling grapes to Australian wineries that we don't know about. We've got no control over that and there is a concern that if something has, say, 20 per cent of Marlborough fruit in it, it could end up labelled as a Marlborough wine. We have spent a lot of time and effort in building up our reputation and we would hate it to be destroyed.'

She was one of many pressing for strict labelling laws which would force wine companies to specify the amount of regional juice within the wine, especially as Marlborough Sauvignon Blanc was being hailed as one of the greatest wine discoveries of the twentieth century by renowned British wine commentator Oz Clarke. There were still some, though, who had to be convinced that this region wasn't getting too big-headed. In 1990 Radio New Zealand interviewed Oz about the importance of Marlborough as a wine producer. The question put to him by the interviewer was: 'Is it true that Marlborough is now acknowledged as one of the world's leading wine regions or is this an antipodean whopper?'

Oz responded: 'No, it's not a whopper, it really isn't. The great thing about Marlborough is that it produced for the first time since the war, maybe the century, a flavour which no one has ever found before. Marlborough's flavour is unbelievably strong, unbelievably memorable. And so long as people go on making the wine like that in Marlborough, it should be a whopping success, especially in European markets because we've been starved of really strong flavours over here for about 600 years. You're getting a flavour of wine which is quite unmistakable, which is unrepeatable so far anywhere else in the world.'

While Oz was lauding Sauvignon Blanc, the Marlborough region was also producing some fine examples of Pinot Noir, Riesling, Chardonnay and sparkling wine. By 1990, Hunter's had expanded their portfolio to eight different varieties and production was reaching 35,000 cases. It had been a period of steady growth and success, but vintage this year was about to throw Jane her first real curveball. Crops were much larger than initially expected, and then the region was hit by a severe autumn frost. John Belsham says it was as though someone had blowtorched the entire Wairau Valley. 'We had never had an autumn frost, or at least not one as severe as this. There wasn't a green leaf left in the valley. We had harvested half of the fruit already, but still had some of our best fruit out there. There was a huge demand on mechanical harvesters as everybody was racing to get the fruit in as soon as possible. Then it started to rain and all those dead leaves began falling off the canopy and attaching themselves like glue to the grapes. There was no longer any decision left, we had to harvest everything right there and then.

Normally you have about three or four days grace after a frost and then the vine starts to shut down, but with the rain, we didn't even have that time period. I don't think I went to bed for three days. It was chaos.'

The severity of the frost was a wake-up call for everyone, and one the doomsayers were quick to grab at. It wasn't unusual at this time to hear people comparing the wine industry with the kiwifruit industry, which had undergone a massive boom-then-bust cycle. Anyone thinking of planting grapes was bound to run into a so-called expert on the industry who would vehemently suggest they put their money elsewhere. More importantly, the impact of the frost, on top of what had been big crops, meant the wines weren't as spectacular as they had previously been, Jane says.

'We were in London to release the new vintage on the rooftop of New Zealand House. We had all these wine writers and buyers there and they were obviously unimpressed with what we were showing them. They had all come to expect great things from our wine; instead they were disappointed. People were saying "Oh, it's gone off the boil. What's happened?" In reality it was because we hadn't learnt how to manage the vineyards with such a big crop. The resulting wines were bland in comparison to earlier vintages. That was a major wake-up call for all of us.'

Another wake-up call was the discovery of phylloxera

in the Hunter's vineyards. Reaction from other growers in the province was severe. To this day people talk about going to functions and being made to brush down their clothes, take their shoes off and empty their pockets, just in case they were inadvertently carrying remnants of phylloxera. Phylloxera is a dreaded grapevine disease. It spreads quickly, there is no cure and no matter how much time and effort is spent on the vines they will eventually die. The only solution is to remove the infected vines and replant with tolerant rootstock. It's understandable there was such fear, as phylloxera was an expense no grower wanted to experience. Since the first discovery in 1984 there had been no further signs emerging in the province. Researchers, however, were insistent that phylloxera was widespread in Marlborough. John Belsham says he was stunned when a viticulturist consultant friend of Tony Jordan's came to visit. 'I was feeling somewhat self-important at that stage and felt I was an instant expert in viticulture. I had had this ongoing debate with the viticulturist about the level of irrigation. I was adamant he was over-irrigating and I didn't want a big leafy canopy. I got the authority from Jane to be able to manage the irrigation and was pretty proud of the way the vines were looking. Then we had this visit from Tony's friend who was a viticultural consultant in Mornington Peninsula. We were walking round the vineyard and I was explaining to him the good canopy balance, feeling rather proud. He said, "These vines look a little stunted to me. You don't think you've got phylloxera do you?" I was quite stunned and said no, there is no phylloxera in Marlborough.'

Slightly abashed at the remark about stunted vines, John was to remember the consultant's comments a few months later when Dr Richard Smart, an internationally acclaimed consultant, arrived at Hunter's to test for phylloxera. He brought with him a number of students, who were set the task of digging up around the roots of the vines to look for the aphids. 'It was autumn, which is the best time to look for phylloxera,' John says. 'At this stage the vines grow another flush of roots as a mechanism to set up for winter. So you have these nice juicy roots very close to the surface and the phylloxera come up to feed off them, which means they are easier to see. I can still remember that day. I was cleaning up at the winery and Richard and his students came round the corner. He was telling me the bad news but at the same time he was so excited because he had just made a scientific discovery. When I look back on those times, I think how naive can one be? You think you are under control, things are going really smoothly and all of a sudden something like phylloxera upsets everything.'

It was a major setback for Hunter's and the rest of the province. Marlborough's Grape Growers Association commissioned a survey of the plains and discovered phylloxera was prevalent and spreading. Knowing how badly the growers had reacted in 1984, Jane took the proactive step of using her vineyard as a teaching source. 'I thought I should bring people in and have a field day. It meant we could show growers what phylloxera-ravaged vines looked like, what they should look for and also show that it was not a disease that instantly destroyed the vines. You could still run a vineyard.'

But it didn't shelter her from rural prejudices. A significant number of growers would not allow machinery that had been working in Hunter's vineyards to be used in their own. And signs declaring Phylloxera-Free Vineyard began appearing on fences throughout the province as growers and companies tried to prevent the spread. In the end it was of no use. Phylloxera was present throughout Marlborough and no talk or sign was going to contain it. While it was a financial disaster for some growers, the eventual impact of phylloxera was positive, Jane says. 'In hindsight it was a godsend. We pulled out all our Bactobel clone of Pinot Noir and replanted with clones of Pinot Noir for table and sparkling wine. We did the same with other varieties, taking the opportunity to replant with quality clones. Admittedly, it was an absolute trauma at the time, but something good came out of it.'

Besides the financial cost of replanting, phylloxera also impacts on production. While the vines can continue to produce for a number of years after being infected, cropping levels and flavours are compromised. Replanting with phylloxera-tolerant rootstock isn't an overnight answer either, as the vines take three years before they will yield anywhere near a reasonable crop. Hunter's began a replanting programme of a few hectares at a time but even so, with the export orders pouring in, a drop in yields was the last thing the company needed.

As if that wasn't enough for Jane to deal with, Hunter's was also being audited by the Inland Revenue Department (IRD). Having just sorted out the legal ramifications of Ernie's very basic will, Jane also had to suffer the ignominy of having to deal with an in-depth investigation into the finances of the company. Mark Peters says the timing couldn't have been worse in a business sense. 'It was a time when everything was squeaky clean and there were a lot of other important things that the business needed to be focusing on, such as getting Hunter's back on a financial footing. We had just started to get things going and putting in place plans and structures that Jane felt comfortable with. The last thing we needed as a distraction was having to focus on an IRD audit. It was incredibly disconcerting.'

The process continued to drag on and it was more than a year before the investigation was complete. Mark says for the entire twelve months, the audit was never far from anyone's mind. 'We were trying to encourage the department to complete it, but they kept coming back to us saying they were short-staffed. What that meant was, we would receive a raft of questions, which I would answer. Then it would go into abeyance for another two or three months, before they would come back to us with another list of questions, relating to the answers I had given months earlier. So I would have to go back through all the papers once again, and try to remember where it was the original answers had come from. I tried to keep Jane out of it as much as possible, but inevitably I would have to ask her for further details.'

At the end of twelve months, the IRD declared there was nothing wrong with the way the company had been run, and besides two extremely minor issues, gave the company a clean bill of health. Decades on, Mark still wonders why it was at this stage in the company's evolution it was deemed necessary to investigate Hunter's. 'I have to question whether or not it was a tip-off from someone, who had intimated something illegal was going on. It was just an entirely frustrating process, that personally I didn't think was necessary.'

Chapter 12

Decanting

*Separating the sediment from wine by
pouring it from a bottle into a decanter*

For years after she took on the role as head of Hunter's Jane would privately second-guess every decision she made. When faced with a difficult situation, whether it be dealing with frost, phylloxera or less than complimentary reviews, she couldn't stop herself from asking, 'What would Ernie have done if faced with the same circumstances?'

Interestingly, it was while addressing a political meeting that Jane bared her soul about the difficulty of life without Ernie.

'When my husband Ernie died in 1987 my whole world came to a sudden stop. On top of the personal grief, I had the dilemma of what to do with his company. Hunter's was very much Ernie Hunter. His personality and his energy had been such that the business seemed like an empty shell without him. How on earth could that be filled? Most people expected it to just wither and die. Some thought it was going to be cruel to prolong the inevitable and a quick sale should be made to capitalise on the name and assets while it still had something of that left. But it seemed wrong for me to walk away, to let Ernie's energy be wasted. I decided to take what Ernie had started and make it succeed. I knew what Ernie's long-term plans were for the company. But when I first sat at the desk upstairs in the little office and gained sufficient overview to realise the enormity of what I was taking on, I realised that the first step was to engage competent people in the various areas of expertise that I needed.

'While I was coming to grips with all this, I ran the company on a footing of cash-flow only, no borrowings. This made sure I wasn't extended, but it certainly limited growth. In hindsight it was the right decision.

'The marketing of the company itself has been a very interesting exercise. As I said before, Ernie was Hunter's wines. The whole company was imbued with his own very masculine personality. A conscious decision was made to change the public perception of the company's personality. Because we are small, it was agreed that personalities are important and particularly useful when marketing domestically and internationally. Consequently, I became a marketing instrument. When I was at first reluctant about this, my PR people said it wasn't the decision for Jane Hunter the ordinary person to make, but for Jane Hunter the managing director.

'I didn't realise how difficult it would be. Not because I was stepping into a man's shoes. Not because I was having to wheel and deal and negotiate and learn very, very fast. But at the end of the day I couldn't enjoy the satisfaction of succeeding. Not the big successes, not even the little successes. To have enjoyed them would have been to usurp what I felt was a success that belonged to Ernie. It is only now, after three years of hard work, that I can accept a feeling of success for myself, when I know that I have done something well, or have achieved something. The company now has enough of my personality in it for me to feel comfortable with identifying with those successes.

'There's not a day when I don't remember Ernie and often I think about how he would have gone about making a decision on a specific matter, but it no longer stops me from deciding for my own reasons, on my own terms, and accepting responsibility for both the successes and failures of those decisions. This personal dilemma of mine, the difficulty of accepting credit for success, has been a trial. A lot of women who are widowed must face the same decision. There are too many factors that come into each and every such situation for me to generalise for others. But I can say to those who decide to pick up the ball and run with it, I'm pleased I did what I did. The trials were worth it. I wouldn't like to be sitting on a veranda somewhere else, looking at the sunset over someone else's grapes, thinking I'd walked away from the chance to make something of the foundation that Ernie and I had put down as a couple.

'I read a very interesting article by Alan Jones late last year. He said he enjoys the concept of success more than that of winning. I liked that and it seemed to put my own business philosophy into a simple phrase. Winning as such implies achieving at the expense of others. Being successful is less to do with cut and thrust and getting on top. It's to do with being pleased with how you are utilising your opportunities, your own skills. Winning is a very transitory thing; success is based on permanence and success does not have to be at the expense of others. I like the idea of being successful rather than winning. Of achieving with other people, rather than at their expense and that has been the pleasure that the wine industry has been able to offer me.

'In preparing my talk tonight I found myself thinking of my own relationship with my memories. How I had these daunting obligations as a widow to respect my husband's memories and not take away from his successes. And then came the realisation that I was entitled to feel good about my own achievements and successes, to set my own goals and make my own mistakes. Achievements are probably the result of treating adversity as a stepping stone, rather than a stumbling block.'

The delivery of this speech was almost a salve to her grief. Once given, she never again publicly spoke of her anguish or her fears of taking on the managing director's role. It was almost as though she had put the insecurities behind her and moved forward. Which was just as well because she was about to be hit with another blow, when winemaker John Belsham announced he was leaving Hunter's to establish his own business. John had been with the company since 1986 and in that time he, along with Tony Jordan, had helped create a range of consistently good wines and provide stability within the company. Jane now had to hire a replacement who didn't mind working for a woman and could get along with Tony to produce and enhance the reliable wines for which Hunter's had become renowned. The word was put out and a number of applicants made contact with Tony. In the end it was an Australian, Gary Duke, who was offered and accepted the role. He had been the assistant winemaker at Hanging Rock Winery in Macedon, Victoria, which is very much a cool-climate region, cooler he says than Marlborough. The vineyard supplying Hanging Rock had been developed in 1987 with the specific goal of producing sparkling wines and Sauvignon Blanc. His experience in both varieties was not lost on Tony Jordan or Jane, whereas Gary himself saw the Hunter's winemaking job as a chance to step up and increase his experience. He arrived with the sole intention of making some of the world's best white wines, supported totally by the management team. He knew little of Hunter's itself but was more than aware of the consistency of the region's wines and enamoured of the fruit being grown in Marlborough. Once on the scene he revelled in the constantly warm and dry conditions that preceded vintage. Warm dry days and cooler nights are a hallmark of Marlborough's autumn weather and 1991 was proving no exception.

'That first vintage the weather was very kind to us. We were able to pick the fruit when we liked due to no worries about rain or frost. It wasn't a big crop, it was just right and well balanced with good natural fruit acidity. I thought to myself, "This is easy."'

Gary wasn't the only newcomer on the Hunter's work front. He was joined by Jane's brother-in-law Peter Macdonald — always referred to as Mac. Married to Jane's older sister Libby, Mac had been convinced to throw in his teaching career in Australia and move out to Marlborough with Libby and their son James. Having spent a Christmas with Jane, the couple could see that while she appeared to be coping with the strains of running a business, she wasn't coping personally. Jane herself says she had hit the wall emotionally. 'I don't think I ever confronted Ernie's death for about three years. I had been so busy that I never seemed to have the time to think about it. Or maybe I didn't want to think about it. But in 1990, when I was under a great deal of stress, especially after the hiccup with vintage, I decided I needed to see a doctor. It was him who sat me down and pointed out that I had not taken time to confront what had happened. He told me I needed to do that.'

It was easy for the doctor to say that but difficult for Jane to follow through, given she was still the only member of the management team on the spot. Realising she was stretching herself too thinly, she offered Mac a job as her right-hand man, something he and Libby didn't need to think about for long. They had been involved in the wine industry back home, albeit on an outside level. They had shares in a crushing facility in the Riverland, near Jane's father's vineyard. The company would bring in fruit from the surrounding area, crush, clarify and refrigerate it, before transporting the juice to the Barossa Valley for production. This minor involvement whetted Mac's appetite. 'Libby's mum Lynne and her husband Brian had a vineyard and small winery in the Barossa Valley, in Lyndoch. I had helped out in the cellar door during holidays and I really enjoyed it. I loved talking about wine and meeting people, so the idea of working in the wine industry wasn't unattractive.'

Libby, Mac and James arrived in Marlborough at the beginning of 1991, the same week as Gary. Straight off, Mac was thrust into the deep end of the job — one that Jane says never originally had a title. 'I don't think I ever gave him one. He always said that he had to do all the things I didn't like — which I said was just about everything.'

Jane admits it can't have been easy sometimes for Mac. Working for your sister-in-law throws up a number of tricky scenarios, not the least family dynamics. Being related didn't always mean you agreed, according to Mac. 'She was irascible and fiery back then and still is to a lesser degree now. But if she fires up it is all over in an instant and then it's back to normal. We get on very well because we can accept that's what happens. I guess if I had to say she had a weakness it would be that she is emotional and can make snap decisions based on emotion. But I understand that and she does too now. And she has a warm side that other people probably don't see. She is compassionate, caring and very loyal.'

Jane describes herself as holding her temper for just so long before it gets the better of her. 'I know I have a temper. I let things go and go and go and then I explode sometimes without warning and often out of context. There have been numerous arguments with people over the years but I don't think I hold a grudge — although they may!'

Mac's involvement in the company provided Jane with some breathing space. She was able to take a step back from doing everything and concentrate on looking at the company, where it had come from and, more importantly, where it was going. It wasn't only in the business sense that she began to feel more relaxed. Having family around her, particularly her sister Libby and nephew James and soon-to-be-born Edward, was a major bonus. Family is all-important to Jane and she has strong loyalties to her parents and her sisters. When Libby and Mac bought their first Marlborough home two streets behind Jane's renovated cob cottage, they provided her with a chance to feel part of a family with children. Meals were shared on a regular basis and her devotion to her nephews was apparent for all to see. 'She absolutely dotes on those boys,' friend Sarah Morphew Stephen says. 'There isn't anything she wouldn't do for them.'

As the boys grew up they spent more than the occasional weekend with Jane. They became like her own children and it is a credit to both Libby and Mac that they allowed her to feel such. She has played a major role in their lives since they were babies and even now she champions their cause in any way she can.

Perhaps the greatest advantage of having Mac working alongside her was that Jane was now able to share the load in terms of management and eventually the marketing. He was also instrumental in ensuring she took better care of her health. 'I don't believe I have ever been good at taking breaks. I certainly didn't for those first three years.

But Mac told me I had to block out two weeks every three months and go away to Adelaide or somewhere. I began to do that. It meant I always knew I had a break coming up and in the long run that really helped me.'

When Mac joined the company, staff levels at Hunter's were nine in total: four in production and five in administration. Jane owned sixteen hectares of vineyard and had six contract growers, many of whom are still growing for her nearly twenty years later. Her steady but slow growth was reflected in the region. The number of wineries was increasing, with Nautilus, Vavasour, Daniel Le Brun, Merlen, Te Whare Ra, Montana, Corbans, Highfield, Grove Mill and Hunter's making wines in the province. Other major companies like Delegat's (who were producing Oyster Bay), Villa Maria, Matua Valley, Selaks Wines (Kumeu) Ltd, Nobilo, Babich and Coopers Creek had contracted growers or had bought land to ensure grape supply. John Belsham's new venture, Vintech, was getting off the ground and it heralded a change in the dynamics of Marlborough's wine industry. Vintech was a contract winemaking operation, which was an entirely new concept for New Zealand, and John says there was an obvious need for such a facility. 'The region was extremely bullish at the time as so many companies were sourcing out of Marlborough and others had bought and planted vineyards. My aim was to establish a facility where I could provide expertise to make wine. But I underestimated the need. First I approached ten major companies to see if they would be interested in using such a facility. Nine of them signed up straight away.'

John promoted the business to wine companies on the understanding that they provided the fruit and wine-making decisions and he would provide the winemaking expertise. Concentrating on quality bottled wines rather than bulk, the majority of product was destined for the export market. Initially he believed it would be only the bigger Auckland-based companies that would want to utilise Vintech's services. He hadn't allowed for the many growers who had been harbouring a desire to establish a label of their own. Chris and Phil Rose, who had been growing for Montana and Hunter's, were one of those to look at expanding into winemaking. Their ensuing wine label, Wairau River Wines, was one of the earlier partners in Vintech. Other companies to emerge from John's development are now some of the biggest in the Marlborough region. They include Saint Clair, Allan Scott, Forrest Estate, Cairnbrae, Lawson's Dry Hills and Jackson Estate. In the first year of operation Vintech handled 1000 tonnes of fruit and by 1995 they were processing 5000 tonnes.

Stability within a business is important to the success of it, as is having good gut instincts, as John had found out when he had floated the idea of a contract winemaking facility.

Jane also has that ability to read a situation and, while she claims she is no businesswoman, she openly admits she has good female gut instincts. 'I think females are far better at delegating than males and better at understanding gut instinct. I am very quick at saying yes or no to an idea, I don't prevaricate. You know if an idea is good, or if you are able to work with someone or not. So why deliberate? Mac and Tony would say that I am quite good at coming up with ideas, but not too good at executing them. That's because, basically, I am a lazy person, I can't be bothered with the nitty gritty. I am good at saying, let's do such and such, but I have no interest in doing the detailed work to achieve that.'

Her ability to get the best from her staff also comes from that gut instinct. Many of the current employees have been there well over a decade. Her philosophy is simple: people have a job and a job description. They are responsible for their job and it is not up to the boss to tell them what they have to do every day. 'I think my role is to see they are not being overloaded and redirect or help them work it out. But in the end everyone has a responsibility to do their own job.'

Her partner, Graeme Coates, describes Jane's style of management as being very female. 'By that I mean it has an emotional management structure. Flowers are given out, she takes an interest in her employees' lives. I don't think you ever see that in a male-run company.'

She has never felt as though being a female at the head of a wine company held her back. In fact, she was once interviewed by the BBC's Radio 4 network, who put it to her that she must have had to overcome gender issues to be as successful as she was. 'I couldn't think of any so the interview was in a sense a bit of a waste of time. But if I was honest, being a woman has helped increase Hunter's profile, especially in the UK — it created a point of difference. There was a period in the nineties when every time there was an issue regarding the wine industry, I was the first point of call. If Television New Zealand's leading current affairs presenter Paul Holmes needed a comment, he would ring me; if national magazines were writing about the industry, they would call me. It got to the stage that I was being quoted constantly. In the first instance we did get more publicity than was due to us, probably because of the sympathy vote. The tragic story of how I came to be heading Hunter's always followed me around early on — but that was a long time ago. I think people can now look beyond that and acknowledge that I am more than a grieving widow following in her husband's footsteps.'

Chapter 13

Pressing

*Applying pressure to the grapes
to remove juice or wine*

Mother Nature is an uncompromising and capricious colleague to work alongside. One minute she is offering you the perfect weather conditions — long, warm, dry days that are a grapevine's Mecca. The next she is throwing rain, frosts and cloud at you in a fit of pique. It is the accepted bane of anybody involved with products off the land that you can only do so much and then the weather gods take over. Marlborough is luckier than most when it comes to having the right climatic conditions for wine production. The long, warm, dry autumns play an important role in developing the unique flavours that the resulting wines are imbued with. Regardless of that, it is hard for anyone to say the region has ever had a perfect vintage. In fact, Jane would go so far as to question whether there is such a thing.

'We had a great year in 1989; 1991 also came pretty close. Then again, so did 2004 and 2007. In 2004 it was a low-cropping year, because we had suffered a severe frost the year before. Our 2004 Riesling was held back from release because it was an absolute stunner. In 2007 even Gary said it was pretty good and from him that is very high praise. But then again, while it was almost perfect for our Sauvignon Blanc, our Merlot suffered, so it's hard to call it perfect across the board. I know Gary loved that first year he was here, as 1991 produced some fantastic wines.'

So much so he wasn't keen to rush the release of the vintage. He knew they had something special with the fruit and was keen to leave the wines in the tank as long as possible. 'It comes together better if you leave them in the tank and don't bother with them. They will be better in the bottle for that time left untouched.'

Jane and Mac had other ideas — they wanted to get this special wine out into the marketplace. 'It got to the stage that I said to Gary, "If you don't bottle some wine soon you are not going to get paid."'

According to Gary that wasn't a one-off comment. 'She says that to me every year.'

If a perfect vintage is calculated by the number of awards bestowed on it, then 1991 was certainly right up there. Taking the hint from Jane, Gary finally bottled the wine just in time to enter it in the Air New Zealand Wine Show. Talk about leaving it until the last minute — the wine was bottled just ten days before the show deadline, yet it still gained a gold medal. Six months later Jane received notification that the same wine had taken out the top award at the Sunday Times Wine Club in London, the same event Hunter's had won three years in a row in the mid-1980s. Despite the obvious thrill at having won, Jane was mystified. In fact, she didn't take the fax seriously when it arrived on her desk, thinking someone was playing an April Fool's Day gag. Hunter's hadn't been back to the competition since Jane had picked up the company's third win in 1988. What she was unaware of was her UK agent Andrew Hamilton had taken it upon himself to enter two Hunter's wines, the 1991 Sauvignon Blanc and the 1990 Chardonnay, in the competition. In much the same way as had happened in the 1980s, the wines fought against each other for top honours. In the first session of the show the Sauvignon Blanc scored a silver medal and the Chardonnay a bronze. In the second session the Sauvignon Blanc stood out, winning a gold medal, and did the same in the third session, while the Chardonnay was awarded silver. When all the scores were totalled, Hunter's had won the trophy for best Sauvignon Blanc and also the trophy for white wine of the show. Jane says there is nothing like being awarded a major trophy, except being awarded one at a competition you had no idea you had entered. There were celebrations all round at the winery and Gary's desire to make the best white wines in the world was proving a little too easy. There was more in store for this wine, however, as it went on to win the Marquis de Goulaine trophy for Best Sauvignon Blanc in the world at the International Wine and Spirits Competition in London. A trophy here is highly sought after. Marlborough was making quite a name for itself at the competition, given a Sauvignon Blanc from the region had been awarded the trophy for two years running. In 1990 Montana won; in 1991 Oyster Bay picked up the top award. Hunter's were the third Marlborough, New Zealand winner in 1992. Thankfully for Jane, being at the awards didn't require any Oscar-style speeches. All she had to do was walk onstage, shake hands with the president of the competition and collect the massive glass trophy.

'It was still a bit daunting though and the trophy itself wasn't the easiest thing to carry home. In fact, the Penfolds Australia guys had won a whole heap of trophies and as they left the hall that night a couple of them slipped on the wet steps. Two of the trophies were dropped and smashed. It made me hold onto mine a little tighter.'

The story of Hunter's win made national news and once again New Zealanders were lapping up the acknowledgement. 'I remember coming back and going through customs and this guy came up to me and said,

"Hey, well done. I saw you on the news last night." I was amazed at the reaction. It was the third year in a row that a New Zealand wine from Marlborough had won, and New Zealand has won it nearly every year since then. But back then getting the hat-trick was pretty special.'

But for every near-perfect vintage there are those that aren't remembered so favourably. Following on from the stunner of 1991, a cataclysmic occurrence thousands of kilometres north-west of New Zealand provided a sobering note for the Marlborough wine industry. The Mount Pinatubo eruption was the second-largest volcanic eruption of the twentieth century, and while it wasn't felt in New Zealand, within six months it was obvious that the release of poisonous gases during the nine-hour eruption was influencing weather patterns the world over. Within two weeks the aerosol cloud had spread around the earth and within twelve months it had covered the planet. The cloud of gases could not disperse quickly, in fact it stayed covering the earth for more than two years, reflecting sunlight away back into space. The end result was a cooling in world temperatures. On average, the Pinatubo eruption is thought to have decreased the mean world temperature by between 0.4 and 0.5 °C. In Marlborough the impact was even worse, with the mean yearly temperature dropping by close to 1.5 °C. That may not seem like much, but for grape growers it was a dramatic drop. Lower temperatures, combined with a cloud base that wouldn't dissipate, meant a significant drop in the all-important growing degree days (an agricultural term that, when applied to grapes, indicates the accumulation of hours when the temperature exceeds 10 °C). That caused a slowing down in the ripening of the fruit. It set back harvest dates in both 1992 and 1993, exposing the growers to the ever-increasing threat of frost.

Mac says there were far more of those during this two-year period and the region had to learn to cope with climatic conditions previously not experienced. 'People were having to learn about viticulture as they went along during that time. We all had a lot of trouble getting the fruit ripe and it cut back our production.'

Hunter's goal had been to increase to 500 tonnes of fruit by 1992. Gary says that was no longer achievable. 'I think it took us about five years to actually achieve that. Pinatubo really impacted; the cool conditions affected the acid levels because the vines weren't getting the sunshine they needed. We had leaf shading and cloud cover, which meant a shorter ripening period. Those wines in 1992 and 1993 had a very different structure from the 1991 wines, as there was more acidity. We had to learn how to remove acid from the wine, which up until that stage they never taught you in school. It was a huge learning curve for all of us.'

The worst year in Marlborough's history, though, wasn't due to a far-away eruption. It was a more basic issue — too much rain. The year 1995 will go down in the history books as the turning point for the industry. Marlborough had basked in typical summer conditions, crops were high, the fruit was looking fantastic and there was a lot of excitement about the upcoming harvest. Until February. Mac remembers being in Australia and ringing back to the winery to talk to Gary. 'He said it's started raining and it's heavy. I sort of laughed it off and told him not to worry, it wouldn't last long. It never does at that time of year. But it just kept raining. Then when it wasn't raining you had this damp, warm cloud coming down from the north. Throughout the rest of New Zealand it was quite sunny, but here in Marlborough we had this blanket of cloud hanging over us for weeks on end.'

Normally rain in Marlborough is followed by long periods of fine conditions with the prevailing nor'westerly winds drying the fruit out. But not in 1995. The sun just never managed to make it out from behind the cloud bank covering the region. If Jane was ever reminded of her earlier statements as a student that she didn't want be involved in the wine industry, this year was it. 'It was one of the worst seasons ever and it was tough work. We were constantly having to walk the vines and find ways of exposing the fruit to whatever sunshine we managed to get.'

The crops were large in 1995, the first time they had been above average for four years. But those bumper crops which had been initially lauded were creating problems of their own. It was becoming increasingly difficult for the fruit to ripen, which wasn't helped by the exponential growth of the canopies due to all the rain. As a viticulturist Jane knew they had no choice but to leaf pluck and trim on a constant basis in an effort to open the canopy up for the fruit to gain exposure. 'We were doing that just about every second day. We also deep-ploughed along the rows to try to get the roots to take up more water and dry out the soil.'

Disease threat was also a major issue. In warm and moist conditions two serious diseases thrive. Downy mildew, which is a fungus, spreads during the appropriate conditions. The white downy growth covers the ripening leaves, eventually causing them to turn brown and die. Botrytis, also known as bunch rot or grey rot (different to botrytis in its finest form, which is known as *Botrytis cinerea* and helps produce sweet dessert wines), is the other disease that Marlborough growers fear. In moist conditions the brown fungal mould settles on the fruit, causing it to become first soft and watery and later causing the berries to shrivel and drop off. While there may only be one or two of the berries infected at first, it can spread very quickly, damaging entire bunches. The impact on fruit quality cannot be underestimated as it imparts a very distinctive musty odour and flavour which is impossible for the winemaker to counter. Marlborough doesn't normally suffer from botrytis infections due to its dry climate. But in 1995 the big dry had been replaced by constant moisture and there were very few vineyards in the province not affected. As the conditions continued throughout March and April, the workload for Jane and the winemaking team intensified.

'I remember we spent lots of time out in the vineyards pulling diseased and rotten bunches off the Sauvignon Blanc. It was grey rot, meaning the fruit was useless. Then we couldn't ripen the fruit because of continuing grey, damp weather, we never seemed to get the Brix [sugar levels] above fifteen or seventeen. Usually we get them up to twenty-two.'

By Easter, which was the middle of April, the conditions hadn't improved. The rains that had been a constant source of irritation since February had one last flourish. Two days before the Easter break, the rain began in earnest and didn't abate for a week. This was no minor shower, it was torrential. Every grower and winery in the province knew they had to get their crops in — fast — if they wanted to salvage anything. The only problem was that the infrastructure wasn't available to cope with the increase in production. As Mac explains, knowing you had to get the fruit in and being able to do so were two completely different scenarios. 'We had problems getting trucks and a harvester as everybody was thinking the same thing. There just wasn't enough machinery to cope with the whole province. We had major problems getting our fruit picked. I remember we had to hand-pick our Malbec in the Awatere Valley and we were literally having to systematically go through the vines and pick what was good fruit and leave all the rotten bunches on the vine and there were a fair few of those.'

A sense of desperation began creeping in as growers and viticulturists frantically tried to track down machinery to get their crops off. Those with the machinery were hounded by those wanting to use it. Wine companies played off against each other, growers the same and friendships in some cases were pushed to the limit. But as tempers frayed, the rain kept on falling, adding to the ever-mounting concerns of the industry. The issue of securing a truck and a harvester at the same time was complicated as vineyard conditions became more challenging. Many growers had cultivated between the rows earlier in the season, exposing bare dirt, which had quickly turned to slushy, clogging mud with the heavy rain. Bad enough for those walking — chaotic for mechanical harvesters used to having solid ground beneath their tyres. As if the pressures weren't high enough for the drivers they now had to deal with being bogged down, sometimes for long periods. Tasks that in normal conditions would take two hours were now taking double that time. Then there was the issue that some companies that had managed to get their fruit off were tying up trucks for hours on end because they couldn't get the fruit into the winery. There were rumours that some people were parking their trucks in front of wineries and leaving them locked up, to ensure their fruit was dealt with before anyone else's. Hunter's weren't saved from the problems, despite having their own winery. Mac says they faced difficulties tying machinery needs together. 'Such as when we managed to get a harvester, we couldn't get a truck. Then when we got a truck, we didn't have the harvester.'

As for the fruit — it wasn't a pretty picture. 'I remember we were just pouring juice down the drain. Trucks would come in and a lot of the free run was useless as the continual rain had swollen the berries and diluted flavours, so we just tipped it out.'

Hunter's ended up paying some growers to leave their rotten fruit on the vines. 'There was no point in bringing it in,' Jane says. 'It would have cost us more to try to harvest it and put it through the winemaking process than it did to pay the growers to leave it there. But we honoured our contracts, because we knew how difficult financially it was going to be for them.'

She jokingly told Gary the bad year was all his fault. 'He came over here from Australia and said he was going to make the best Sauvignon Blanc in the world. Well, he hit it in 1991. Then we had 1992, which was only okay, then 1993 which was terrible, 1994 was good but 1995 was a disaster.'

As well as a lack of machinery, wineries were faced with a lack of storage space. Normally the fruit comes in in batches, allowing the winemaker to work systematically. But in 1995, with everything coming in at once, there weren't enough tanks to hold all the juice. Milk tankers, brewing tanks and massive plastic receptacles were all employed as temporary holding facilities.

The repercussions of the 1995 vintage would be felt for a long time after the rain finally ended. Mac says it changed the entire infrastructure of the Marlborough wine industry. 'We changed our focus after that year. We invested in a machine harvester and formed an agreement with one of the freight trucking companies in case it ever happened again. Basically we never wanted to be caught out the way we had been in 1995.'

Gary says at the time he wanted to be doing anything other than trying to make wine. 'I would have liked to be the lollipop man on the road during that time. It was the vintage from hell and touch wood we haven't had one since, but there is always the potential.'

Marlborough's first grapes had only been planted twenty-two years earlier and in that short time-frame the region had gone from being an unknown to New Zealand's most important producer. The region had achieved international acclaim and was recognised as a significant New World producer. On top of all the hype, the number of individuals who were keen to have their own little slice of the industry had also grown. For many of them it was their first experience of the vagaries of agriculture. It's not cheap to establish a vineyard and many were relying on their 1995 crop to pay back large debts. With wineries unable to harvest all the fruit, or in some cases actually leaving crops on the vines, growers were unable to recoup their costs. There were a number of situations where growers ended up suing the company they had contracted their fruit to in an effort to compensate for their loss of income. Wineries themselves were facing an abundance of fruit that didn't reach the high standards they had set. The resulting wines could not possibly match the quality benchmarks that had been achieved in previous years. If ever the Marlborough wine industry was facing breaking point, this was it. A few months after harvest there was a rush of small vineyards up for sale as growers began feeling the financial pressure. Vintage also impacted on some of the smaller wineries, which had had difficulty getting their fruit processed. After three years of smaller crops, companies had been hoping to increase production in 1995. Instead, many were faced with a lack of production, or worse still, wines that weren't up to the quality standards they had established.

There is only one other year that came anywhere close to the trauma of 1995 and that was 2003, when the region was hit by one of the worst spring frosts on record. Large tracts of vineyard throughout the Wairau Plains and further afield were hit by plummeting early-morning temperatures just as the vines were bursting into flower. Frost at this stage in the vine's cycle kills off the leaves and burns the emerging fruit flower, leaving the vines with reduced crops. The end result is small yields and in the wineries' case, diminished production.

Adding to the pressure, wineries were also facing higher grape prices as growers sought to buffer their drop in yields with a hike in payments. It was a region-wide problem as companies fell over themselves to get a supply of fruit to meet their commitments. For Hunter's, the policy of always buying more fruit than was actually required paid off and even though the yields were down, the subsequent quality wasn't, Jane says. 'Smaller crops often mean more intense flavours, so the 2004 vintage was something quite special. It was just a shame we didn't have more of it.'

The end result of the frost would see the average grape price for Sauvignon Blanc reach its highest point ever — $2559 a tonne. At the time of writing, that price has not been surpassed.

Chapter 14

Blending

Utilising several batches of wine to
create a more complex end product

Keep your friends close, and your enemies closer, is an old Chinese saying dating back to 400 BC. In Jane's case, the traumas of 1995 added another context to the original quotation. Her father had always instilled in her a belief that you had to keep your bank manager informed, whether the news was good or bad. That way nothing was ever a surprise. Following on from that she strongly believed in letting her distributors around the world know what they were in for, in advance.

If the vintage had been a big one it was better for distributors to know so they had time to open new markets. Likewise, if the vintage had been a small one it was better for them to have advance warning. So it was in 1995 that

Jane contacted her distributors well ahead of bottling to let them know some wines would not be available and, in the case of Sauvignon Blanc, quantities would be less than expected. 'I informed them that we were only going to have half the amount of Sauvignon Blanc we thought we would have and there would be no Riesling and no Oak Aged Sauvignon Blanc.'

She also prepared a press release explaining the reason why Hunter's had decreased production. Sent to distributors and media in the UK, it led directly to one of her darkest periods. 'Basically, I sent it out to let them know we had had a bad year. I explained how Hunter's had suffered due to the weather conditions, which meant we would not be producing certain wine styles this year. Hunter's has always had a policy of producing wines of consistent quality. If we can't do that, we won't release them and that year, due to the amount of bad fruit, we would be reducing our quantities. But in saying that, the Sauvignon Blanc we would be releasing was very good. The press release was only related to Hunter's Wines but unfortunately some people mistook it as Jane Hunter talking about New Zealand wines as a whole.'

She had no comprehension of what a furore her statement would create. Within days there were reports in wine magazines emanating from the UK stating that New Zealand's vintage had been a disaster. Articles about poor fruit quality and a drop in production started filtering back to wine companies back home. The reaction was severe and swift. 'Personally I received a lot of flak from other members of the wine industry. Some of it was extremely personal and certain individuals were vitriolic to say the least. It didn't seem to matter that I had released a press statement that constantly referred to Hunter's and had not in any way referred to the rest of the Marlborough industry and certainly not to the New Zealand wine industry as a whole. It was a turning point for me. I guess I hadn't understood the profile that Hunter's had in the UK market. Because we were one of the first to make our name over there, we were looked upon differently to many other wine producers. Suddenly when we talked about a bad year the media jumped to the conclusion that we were referring to everybody having a bad year.'

While no longer a member of the New Zealand Wine Institute, Jane wasn't immune to the negativity that was coming her way from individual members. For months after her press release it was the topic of conversation around the board table and the strength of feeling against her became very apparent. She was told in no uncertain terms that if she wasn't going to say something positive, then she shouldn't say anything at all. Her response to that was: 'Isn't it better to be honest?'

As for the rest of the industry, it went into overdrive to counter any damaging publicity regarding the 1995 wines. Wine companies sent out their own press releases to distributors around the world disputing the fact the wines from this difficult season weren't up to standard. And they were quite within their rights to do so, as some special wines did come out of 1995, Mac says. 'I was surprised at how good the wines out of 1995 were, even if they weren't our best wines. It says something about the strength of this region, really. The Sauvignon Blancs were still wines you could drink. They certainly weren't throw-down-the-drain wines, they weren't dirty wines — they were okay. Some of the Pinot Noirs didn't last too long, but they also were drinkable. It just shows you there is more to this region than the entrepreneurs or the winemakers. What saved us in that year was the combination of terroir and the varieties we were growing. It could have been a lot worse.'

Jane agrees the vintage wasn't a complete disaster. 'We were delighted with what we picked early in terms of Pinot Noir and Chardonnay for base wines for our sparkling. Our Breidecker, which is an early-maturing variety, was picked without problem and was probably the best we'd ever had; Gewürztraminer wasn't the largest of yields but it was the best quality ever. It was really just our Riesling and Sauvignon Blanc and the late-maturing red varieties that caused problems.'

The negativity had a direct impact on Jane's personal confidence. 'It meant I retreated quite a bit. I have never become involved in wine industry events or functions since then. I just felt I was unfairly targeted. And I have to say it hurt — a lot. From that time on the New Zealand Wine Institute would send out memos highlighting how they would be promoting the vintage. I thought that was totally dishonest and misleading. What gets me is that the French and Italians always come out and say whether they have had a good year or a bad year. What is wrong with us saying that? I always believe it's better to prepare the market and to prepare your distributors ahead of time, rather than lead them up the garden path.'

It wasn't just a case of her pulling back from industry events. Jane noticed that suddenly she wasn't invited to them. For someone who had helped establish the Export Guild and had been involved at a high level of the New Zealand wine industry, the snub was hard to take. Not only was she having to deal with a drop in production that would directly impact on the cash-flow of the company, but she was also having to deal with her sudden exodus from industry favour.

Not everyone took affront. One Marlborough wine industry member who was at the London wine tastings later in 1995, says Jane's stance was much respected by wine writers in the UK. Richard Bowling says some of the other wine companies didn't receive quite the same response. 'I was ashamed with the behaviour of the wine industry trying to tell the English press that nothing had gone wrong. It was a snow job and the press weren't buying it. The British wine trade is the most experienced wine trade in the world and here was this bunch of amateurs from New Zealand trying to say there was nothing wrong with the vintage. One of the top wine writers of the time who I was speaking to, told me that if that happened again New Zealand wouldn't be treated so fairly. Jane was one of the only people at the time to be honest. I gave her enormous credit for that because the behaviour of the industry was shameful. Well, not so much shameful, it was more a case of bringing discredit to the whole New Zealand wine industry. Far more so than Jane telling them her company had been affected by the conditions.'

Jane wasn't the only one learning lessons from the vintage. In her case it may have been not to release press statements — but for the rest of the industry it had become apparent there was a need for a stronger infrastructure in terms of machinery and equipment. For smaller wine companies the need to have control over their destiny, particularly when it came to wine pro-duction, also arose. Gary says there was a move after the 'vintage from hell' for many small companies to finally invest in their own winery. Other companies expanded their facilities to ensure they were never caught without space if another 1995-style year should occur. 'We always made sure we had more than enough capacity, not so we could process more in terms of tonnage, but to ensure we had the tank space to honour our contract growers. In 1995 we had all sorts of not-so-great facilities. We had beer tanks, plastic tanks and milk tanks just to cope with all the fruit. We never wanted to be in that situation again.'

Jane says the dreadful conditions had highlighted the need for growers and wine companies to work more closely together. 'There are some growers who regard themselves only as suppliers of a raw material for which they expect the same or better prices year after year, irrespective of the quality of the grapes or the problems of the winery in recovering the costs of turning those grapes into wine, let alone doing so profitably. The long-term future of the wine industry in Marlborough means grape growers need to make a clear choice between long-term commitment and unrealistic short-term gain.'

Sympathetic to the grower, whose only source of income from the wine industry comes from the sale of grapes to a winery, Jane also believes there are some who just don't see the whole picture. 'Once the grapes are sold that is the end of their involvement — and the end of their risk. From then on the risk is carried by the winery and it's a costly risk. First there's the capital costs of winemaking equipment such as crushers, presses, pumps, centrifuges, oak barrels and other wine-specific items. Then there's the bottling and other packaging equipment required before the wine can be turned into a marketable state. That's followed by warehousing, marketing and distribution costs. These are all factors the winery has to cover financially, after the grapes have been paid for. There are some very good growers who regard themselves as being part of the wine industry and who are willing to share, with the wineries they supply, the risks inherent in the industry. In years such as 1995, where nature intervened to reduce the price a winery could expect to recover from wines made from sub-standard grapes, they accept they won't receive the same price as in a trouble-free year. These growers take the long-term view and accept the commitment to quality and consistency that the wine industry entails. But then there are the other growers, who are only looking to make a quick fortune at the expense of someone else. Personally, I believe these short-term gainers should maybe look at growing another crop that has less emphasis on quality or eventual saleability.'

If there was a bright side to the 1995 vintage it was the innovative production of wines that came out of Hunter's. With a lack of premium quality Sauvignon Blanc juice, the management team came up with the idea of blending two varieties together. It resulted in a Chardonnay/Sauvignon Blanc that was cleverly marketed by Hunter's advertising agency Saatchis as providing the best of both worlds. Then there was the decision to produce a new style of sparkling wine utilising the quality Pinot Noir and Chardonnay fruit picked before the big rain. The company was already producing a sparkling wine, Hunter's Brut, made in a Champagne style utilising Pinot Meunier, Pinot Noir and Chardonnay. The sparkling wine had first been made in 1987 and while it was a tiny portion of the overall Hunter's wine production, it was an extremely popular one. But because the wine spent three-and-a-half years on lees, it was too expensive for the export market.

'If we had sent it to the UK it would have been sitting alongside medium-priced French Champagnes and it would have been too much to expect consumers to try a New Zealand sparkling wine when they could buy a French Champagne for the same price. So we sold it domestically through the trade, mail order and our restaurant.'

A few years earlier Jane had been chatting with Terry Dunleavy, who had been suggesting to the industry at large that they use Maori names to distinguish their wines overseas. One of the names he had come up with was Mirumiru, which is the Maori word for bubbles. 'The industry didn't take to the idea at all but I loved the name Mirumiru. I asked Terry if I could use it and he said go ahead, so I trademarked it as MiruMiru™, capitalising the second M, and held on to it for a few years. In 1995 it seemed the perfect time to bring it out.'

MiruMiru™ is very different in style to the sparkling wines Hunter's had been making up until this point.

'It was a much fruitier and less yeasty style than our Hunter's Brut and it was costing less to produce because it wasn't having to stay on lees so long. We know that when people in the UK think of Marlborough they think intense fruit, so we decided to release MiruMiru™ into that market specifically.'

In appropriate style MiruMiru™ was launched in London at the penthouse of New Zealand House in London in 1997. It was a huge success and within weeks of the launch even the iconic Harrods were stocking it on their shelves. Within a year it was rated as the best new wine in the UK market at the International Wine Challenge Awards. The actual award was the James Rogers Memorial Trophy, which is given to a wine in its first year of release in the UK market. In all the years of the award prior to 1997 a sparkling wine had never won, and neither had any New Zealand wine producer been recognised. The accolades continued when MiruMiru™ won gold at the Wine Magazine International Wine Challenge alongside the likes of Moët et Chandon, Bollinger and Charles Heidsieck. Only seven golds were awarded, six of those to French Champagne houses, the other to Hunter's. Bringing a smile to the faces of the winemaking team was the fact Dom Perignon, Moët's premium Champagne, was awarded silver. Tom Stevenson MW, the author of the *World Encyclopedia of Champagne and Sparkling Wine*, penned a quirky poem for Jane after tasting the wine.

MiruMiru™ on the wall.

Who's the fairest fizz of all?

Hunter's of course.

Hunter's weren't the first company in New Zealand to make the most of the Maori heritage in terms of naming their wines. But perhaps they have been the most successful, which Jane says has something to do with the ease of pronunciation. 'We have only used words that sound just as they are written. MiruMiru™ has a strong appeal throughout New Zealand. It's distinctive and it's easy to say, as we have found out. At the 2008 Wine Festival we had hundreds of people coming up and asking simply for a glass of Miru.' Initially only available in the UK, production has increased and it is now sold throughout New Zealand and other export markets around the world, and Hunter's have changed the name of their Brut sparkling to MiruMiru™ Reserve. While still only limited in terms of quantities, Jane says if Hunter's had had a larger promotional budget they could have accomplished an enormous amount with this wine style. 'Sparkling wine is a product that you have to do a lot of promotional work with. You have to get it into restaurants and get people to drink it. The best way of achieving that is to get the restaurant to pour MiruMiru™ by the glass. But that is hugely expensive — even though it probably saves on other forms of advertising. If we had a bigger base we could have marketed it far more but because we are making smallish quantities we can't compete against the Champagnes or even Montana's Lindauer.'

MiruMiru™ is not the only Hunter's wine adorned by a Maori name. The company also produces Kaho Roa, an oak-aged Sauvignon, and Hukapapa, a dessert Riesling. 'All three of these wines are produced in small quantities and are slightly different. Instead of saying they are winemaker's selections or using a vineyard name for the marketing, we opted to give them Maori names. In the case of the sparkling we felt it was important to give it a unique New Zealand name to take it right away from Champagne.'

Alongside the distinct New Zealand names on the bottles, Jane has also developed a unique environment around the winery. While visitors to the cellar door and restaurant have always been able to wander among manicured gardens and trellised vines, Jane felt it was all becoming a bit overwhelming. A full-time gardener was employed to take care of the cottage garden but even he couldn't prevent the wear and tear caused by Marlborough's strong nor'westerly winds. 'One weekend I left the winery and everything was looking just lovely. The roses were in full bloom, the hydrangeas were out, and there were daisies and lavender everywhere. Then we got this howling wind over the weekend and when I called into work on the Sunday afternoon the place was a mess. Everything was dried up and needed dead-heading. I thought, I have had enough of this. I decided then and there that I would put in a New Zealand native garden.'

Di Lucas from Christchurch was asked to come up with a plan utilising only natives endemic to the area. Flaxes, grasses, ferns, cabbage trees and other natives have taken off in startling fashion, partly watered by waste water from the winery to ensure sustainability. It was a planned transformation of the entire area surrounding the winery and cellar door. 'We don't have the spectacular vista that some wineries here in Marlborough have, but we have endeavoured to create our own little world, very much a slice of New Zealand, instead. A lot of people visiting here don't get the chance to actually get out into the bush in New Zealand, which is such a shame as our bush is very beautiful. We wanted to recreate that here and I think we have succeeded. Walking down that walkway from the car park to the wine shop surrounded by native plants with the birdlife above, it is really lovely. Very calming.'

Even the garden surrounding the restaurant has undergone change. The swimming pool that had attracted families in years gone by was removed and replaced with a garden featuring endangered native plants endemic to Marlborough. Jane is understandably proud of the development. 'It has been amazing to see how well everything has grown. I've discovered that when plants are in their right environment they just take off. Some of the plants that we had were only a few centimetres tall when we planted them. Within a matter of months they were triple that. We could almost see them growing before our eyes.'

Gardening is one of Jane's real loves. While early on she admits she knew little about plants and trees, despite her degree, she has become passionate about her own private garden. 'Gardening calms me down. Early on it was a release for me, even if I didn't know what I was doing. I was one of those people who would see something they liked at the garden shop and buy it without thinking where it was going to go when I got home, or what conditions it needed to flourish. I'd just plant it somewhere and hope for the best. Nothing was ever planned. Even these days it's not, I just like being able to potter. It's a great release.'

Her garden surrounding the cob cottage grew tremendously over the years, providing her with a tranquil release from the rigours of work. But as work took her away from Marlborough for up to four months a year, it all became a bit too much. 'I was paying someone to come in and mow the lawns, someone to keep the pool clean, someone to do the gardens and I wasn't even there much to enjoy it. I decided it was time to sell.'

In 2005 she moved into what at first appears to be a much smaller property in Blenheim. However, looks can be deceiving as the two-storey townhouse provides almost double the space of the cob cottage, and the surrounding grounds provide an array of separate gardens. 'I just love it as it is modern, the house is so much larger and the courtyard gardens are a bit of an oasis. The real beauty of this place is that I can lock it up and go away and not have to worry about it. I just love having that freedom, yet I haven't had to give up my garden to achieve that.'

Chapter 15

Balance

*The harmonious relationship of
all the components of wine*

Wine may flow through Jane's veins but it is definitely animals that capture her heart. She is a big softie when it comes to four-legged companions and Karen Rose isn't the only one to say she intends coming back as an animal, specifically as one of Jane's precious pets. It's not just the attention she lavishes on them, it is the out of the ordinary events she treats them to. Take her cat Sooty, for example. While living in Adelaide he didn't seem to realise that as a feline he was supposed to be content eating, sleeping and chasing the occasional bird or mouse. This short-haired black cat instead adopted the persona of travelling companion to Jane, insisting that everywhere she went, he went. He would think nothing of plonking himself on the floor of her car for the two-hour trip from the city out to the Riverland, where her father lived. His love of travel wasn't confined to just cars. He accompanied Jane to New Zealand when she moved here in 1980 and three years later when she moved to Marlborough Sooty travelled with her perched on her lap, much to the bemusement of fellow passengers. Later he would escort Jane and Ernie to their bach in Penzance Bay, only to go walkabout for the entire time they were staying. 'He had this amazing ability to know when we were getting ready to come home. I wouldn't have seen him for the whole time we were at the bach but as soon as I began to pack up he would reappear.'

After years of having Jane to himself, Sooty had to deal with sharing Jane not only with Ernie, but also with Ernie's first St Bernard, Pinot, and then Commodore. As if that wasn't enough, another addition to the family arrived — Sweep the goat. 'I used to dread it whenever Ernie went away because he always seemed to arrive home with something new. He would leave in one Range Rover and arrive home in a new one. Or one day he came home with a bootload of paintings. Then one night he went out to visit John Stichbury [of Jackson's Estate] and came home with this damn goat. I have no idea why.'

Ernie knew only too well that Jane wouldn't be able to refuse a new pet, even if it wasn't exactly what she expected him to turn up with. Instead, she set about making the Rapaura Road property goat-friendly, getting a hut constructed and fencing off part of the backyard. Sweep, though, believed he was far better than other animals of his ilk and made it his goal in life to escape and invite himself inside. 'I'd be in the kitchen or doing something inside and I'd turn around to find Sweep, Sooty and Commodore all standing there watching me. Thankfully they didn't make any mess.'

Sweep and Commodore had a strong friendship based on play-fighting, with the dog more than happy to take on the goat in a battle of head butting. While quite at home in the garden and inside the cottage, Sweep was also enamoured with the sheep that lived in the paddock next door. He would regularly break his chain and jump the fence for a bit of companionship during the working day, returning only when lured with an apple. When Jane moved to the cob cottage in 1988, she took Sweep with her, only to discover he didn't like being left at home with no human or animal contact for hours on end. He got to the stage where he wouldn't eat, was morose and starting to lose condition. Typical of Jane, she decided he had to be moved to the winery, where he would be surrounded by constant activity during the day. What was to become the most expensive goat pen in Marlborough, Sweep's new home was built right next to the barrel hall. 'He had this huge yard with a fort, a two-tiered condominium made from the packaging from the new press with gang planks, and then we made a massive hill out of dirt so he could run up and down it. Gary always used to say, "Bloody goat, it has the most expensive real estate in the province."'

Even with all the attributes of his designer home, Sweep wasn't confined to it. Jane would often feel sorry for him and let him out to wander around the winery property. Being used to human contact it was too much to expect he would stay put on the grass. There were numerous occasions when visitors to the wine shop would be surprised to find themselves being nuzzled on their behind by this wayward goat. 'He would obviously see all these people coming into the winery and run in to be a part of whatever was going on. It was funny watching people's reactions.'

Commodore's antics were just as legendary. Whenever something or someone new turned up to the winery, they would get the once over from the slobbering dog. Visiting the restaurant was never complete unless the gentle giant had paid a visit and enticed you to offer him a snack or three. Even his propensity to break wind was not enough to put people off. It was not unusual for Commodore to let rip, then stand up and shake himself before walking away from any distasteful lingering scent, leaving the humans racing for fresh air.

But the love of Jane's life would have to be Paddy, who arrived on the scene early in 1992, just a few months after

Commodore died. Following the death of the gentle giant, Jane was adamant she wasn't going to get another dog. No matter how much her friends and employees begged her to reconsider she remained staunch — until she saw the *Crufts Dog Show* on television. 'I was at the Penzance bach with Libby and it was one of those dismal days so we sat down to watch telly. I caught the end of *Crufts*, where they were announcing the winner and there was this amazing-looking dog. It was a Clumber Spaniel and he was playing up to the crowd. Every time they clapped he puffed himself up, he was almost grinning. I was absolutely taken with him. Of course, when I mentioned this to the women at work they all looked at each other and decided to take matters into their own hands.'

Without letting on to Jane they began researching the winning dog and discovered that the parents of the Crufts' Clumber Spaniel were being brought out to New Zealand by their owners. What's more, the bitch was pregnant. The women couldn't wait to tell Jane, who had to admit it was serendipitous. Encouraged by friends and staff she decided to contact the owners of the dogs and enquire about buying one of the ensuing pups. It wasn't just a case of enquiring and paying the money up front; Jane herself was checked out to ensure she would be a suitable owner. Of particular interest to the breeders was whether the dog would be seen by the public. Clumber Spaniels aren't a common breed of dog and with such a distinguished pedigree, the owners wanted the pups to gain exposure. Given how Jane intended taking her dog to work every day, the owners quickly agreed to sell her one.

The next hurdle was finding a name. While he had a kennel name of Gruffyd Bruisyard, the breeders wanted Jane to provide a common name as soon as possible so it could be used from the day he was born. 'I wanted to have an Irish name so everyone had to come up with an idea. We had a huge list of names but either the name didn't seem right or we couldn't agree. I think everyone was getting quite frustrated when Pete McConway came up and said, "Oh Jane, for goodness sake why don't you just call him Paddy?" Oh right. Yes, that makes sense, I thought. And then when he arrived he had this way of walking that seemed like he was padding along. It was just so appropriate.'

Paddy fitted in just where Commodore left off, albeit not in such a large way. At his heaviest he only managed to tip the scales at 45 kg, a good 50 kg less than his predecessor. His personality, though, was massive. Being a spaniel he was intensely food orientated, which was discovered very quickly by both Jane and the rest of Hunter's staff. 'He would wander in each morning and head straight for the lunch boxes of the workers, especially during vintage when our staff numbers increase. There were so many times that one of the workers would be heard yelling in frustration that they had lost their lunch or morning tea after Paddy had helped himself. Every year we had to warn the vintage workers to put their bags up high where he wouldn't be able to reach them.'

He was also an attention-seeker extraordinaire. If the limelight wasn't focused on him he would find some devious way to attract it. 'One night when we were having drinks in the office and Paddy was being ignored by everybody, he wandered off to one of the offices and came back with a mouthful of medal-winning neck tags that were to go on bottles. That ensured we noticed him. Or he would help himself to personal items in people's bags and wander back with them.'

He quickly became the new face of Hunter's, helped out by some clever writing by Ken Hudson, who was producing the Hunter's newsletter. He had established a Saintly Words column when Commodore was alive, writing humorous anecdotes as if they had been dictated by the dog himself. Ken established a Paddy's Place column shortly after Paddy arrived on the scene, where the dog's inability to spell was a major feature. The following introduced this four-legged rascal to the wider Hunter's community.

Hello. My name is Paddy and I don't know a thing about wine. I don't know much about anything really. I'm not very old and I know I've got a lot to learn but being taught stuff is very b-o-r-i-n-g. I'd rather play neat games and stuff. Trouble is, I keep getting shouted at. All the peoples does it. Jane says it is because I am too boystruss (whatever that means). I just like to explore. Every time I do, someone is there to shout at me.

It was a different story when I first got here. I was patted, stroked, smiled at, tickled and everybody (I mean e-v-e-r-y-body) thought I was so-ooo cute they had to say 'aaahh.' Everything was new and boy you don't know how neat it was exploring the whole place for the first time and inventing all these keen games to play. If you've never been to Hunter's I'll tell you what it is really like when you know how to have fun. So let's take a tour together . . .

Wine Shop and Offises

First thing in the morning I usually get taken straight into the wine shop. That's connected by an open door to Jane's offis and another opens into Peter's offis. The whole front of the winery is one long and very warm runway. What's even better, each room has big windows that slide right across, so I can also run in and out of any or all of the rooms. Most visitors come to one or other offis or wine shop so I can run and greet any peoples that come. That's one of the times I get growled at. Especially when Jane is 'in conference' and wants to shut me out. I can make a really neat noise by scratching on the glass with my claws. She gets so-ooo mad!

The other time I get shouted at is when someone is buying some wine in the Wine Shop and I rush in and jump on them and lick their hands and wag my tail and knock over the price cards . . . !

The Winery

The next place to go is the winery itself. That's just behind the ofisses. The peoples in there are generally very friendly — except when a hose has been on recently (which happens quite a lot because it is a very clean place). Then they get positively wary. I think this is because the best way to treat the puddles on the floor is to a) drink a bit, b) run through them quickly, and c) roll in them and shake yourself vigorously — with some peoples nearby if it can be arranged. There is also a lot of empty bottles waiting to be filled. When you knock them over they make a really beaut clatter. I only have to get nears them and the peoples in the winery all start screaming and chase me away. It's a great game.

The Lab

Then there's the labortree, labortary, the not now room. That's where Gary does a lot of strange things with juice, wine and stuff. Gary is a lot of fun in the open air — but when he gets in here all he can say is 'not now Paddy'. I don't know what he gets up to but it sure makes him boring.

Barrel Room

One of the neatest places to run around is the Barrel Room. That's where all the juice and stuff gets to furment into wine. It does this inside these really big barrels which are stacked up from floor to ceiling. It gets nice and dusty behind the barrels and since peoples can't get behind them you can roll around as much as you like and not get shouted at.

Actually, peoples don't go into the Barrel Room much. There's not much for them to do in there. That makes it fun. I can sneak in there and bark and gruff and listen for another dog to do the same thing. Gary says it is an echo. I don't care what breed it is, it's company (of a sort.)

The Restront

The Restront is another fun place to visit sometimes. I pop across there about 20 times a day. There isn't much to do (I'm not even allowed inside) but if you're lucky there is a window around the side and if you bark loudly enough the window opens and a bit of meat pops out. Of course if you bark too loudly, Jane or Peter comes out of their offisses and shouts at me. Behind the Restront there is an area than can only be described as Heaven. It is an area of grass. There are lots of wooden tables there with umbrellas in them. Peoples sit out there with lots of food. They leave a lot of the food. There in the open air, on tables left for a-n-y-b-o-d-y to help themselves to. The only problem is there is a fence around it, so I can't get in. One day I will . . . I must . . . I've just got to . . .

The Trellis

In front of the Winery is the Trellis. This is a whole field of vines that are growing above people-head height. There's plenty of room underneath to walk, run . . . and chase balls. This is a really neat game that Gary started one day shortly after I arrived and he was just as bad as everyone else at patting me and making a fuss and saying 'Aaaah' and stuff. Nowadays Peter and Jane play it too. The game is simple enough. They throw the ball, I chase after it. What makes it extra fun in the Trellis is the way it will bounce off the trunks just as I'm flying after it. I have to wheel around real fast and go in the opposite direction just as the ball has hit another trunk and is flying off in yet another direction. It's neat!

Well that's Hunter's. It's a neat place if you can avoid getting yelled at. Peoples seem to do that pretty much anywhere and at any time. In fact I can't understand why I've got the name I have when they are the ones who keep getting themselves into a paddy. Can you?

Paddy was more than just a dog to Jane. He was her constant companion. Mac says he was considered an equal to his and Libby's two boys. 'There was James, then Edward and then Paddy. He was the third child in the family and was hugely important to Jane.'

'He got me through some really tough times and I don't think I could have been bothered to come to work sometimes if I hadn't had Paddy,' Jane says.

Even when she went away, Paddy was never left alone. A minder came in to look after him at night, and one of the staff would always collect him from home each morning and take him out to the winery for the day, taking him home again at night. 'He never missed a day at work.'

It was almost as if Paddy knew whenever a Hunter's publicity shot was about to be taken. Somehow he managed to inveigle himself into nearly every photo or video involving Jane. 'He pinched all the publicity whenever he could. The last bit we have of him on video, he wasn't supposed to be in. It was a *Destination Travel* series for Air New Zealand Inflight and Paddy was getting quite old. I said to Mac we wouldn't include him in the filming so Mac kept him inside. I wandered off with the presenter and the film crew walking between the vine rows, chatting away. But Mac took Paddy outside for a walk at morning tea and bugger me if Paddy didn't spot us from way down the bottom of the vineyard. Next thing he comes running up towards us and Kelly the presenter said, "What a cute dog. We must have him in the clip." I just thought, Oh God!'

Related to Princess Anne's Clumber Spaniel, Paddy had his fair share of admirers. Due to all the attention he received from visiting media, international visitors were known to make a point of visiting the wine shop just to meet the dog. One Irish couple arrived at the winery one Saturday morning eager to get up close to Paddy, only to be devastated that he wasn't on site that day. Determined they would not return home without the obligatory photo, they drove off to the West Coast and drove back on Monday specifically to see the dog. Presents and letters were arriving on a constant basis, to the point where Jane had to set aside drawers in her office to hold all his toys. He had another huge basket of playthings at home. Fitting into the winery lifestyle, Paddy even made a cautious friendship with Sweep. However, he wasn't keen on sharing the limelight and when children used to visit the winery bringing with them bread for the goat, it all got too much for Paddy. He was caught head first through the fence stealing the bread before Sweep could get to it.

For Jane he was a godsend as a lot of personal attention shifted from her to the dog. Not everyone held the same view. 'Gary used to say, "I'm sick of it. No matter where I go for a wine tasting, whether it's New York, or the UK or Australia, the only thing people want to talk about is Paddy. How is he? What's he up to?" But for me it was fantastic. It took the pressure off me a bit and it was a real ice breaker when it came to talking to strangers.'

In 2006 Paddy died at the age of fifteen, and for the first time since she arrived at Hunter's Wines, Jane no longer had a dog. She admits it would be nigh on impossible to replace Paddy and she has shown no interest in getting another pup. 'He had the most amazing personality that no other dog could measure up to. I now just have the cat that walked into my cob cottage some years back and whom I named Pushie Kat.'

Dogs and wineries go hand in hand these days. There are even best-selling books that focus on canines who have made themselves at home amongst the barrels and tanks. But in Marlborough in the 1980s and 1990s they were a novelty. Pinot, then Commodore and Paddy especially were doggy pioneers.

Another pioneering aspect of Hunter's Wines Ltd was the restaurant. Despite the fact that Jane had vehemently declared she would never have anything to do with the food industry after her stint as a cafe owner in the early 1980s, she had no choice but to support the on-site winery restaurant. Over the years it would prove to be more than a small headache as chefs came and went and she dealt with the fickleness of customers. As more wineries provided eating establishments, Hunter's lost their initial exclusivity. Jane decided it needed some serious revamping. She called on the services of close friend Jeremy Jones, who had been the successful owner of The Peppertree Restaurant on the outskirts of Blenheim, to help with the refurbishing. Moving away from the casual atmosphere, he developed a more sophisticated decor which utilised the company name in terms of hunting paraphernalia. Coinciding with the new look, Jeremy helped establish a Friday Night Club aimed at business people looking for a place to relax after work at the end of the week. Jeremy described it as a 'country club' just ten minutes out of town. Becoming a member gave you a number of privileges, including a discount on all purchases at the wine shop, free entry to the wine bar all year and special invitations to new releases and Hunter's promotional events. The uptake was very strong and within a matter of weeks the Friday Night Club was *the* place to be. Within months it developed further when Grahame Thorne, ex-All Black and parliamentarian, offered to hold a curry night one Friday. He and his wife Briony were renowned in Auckland for hosting such nights at the Globe Hotel. He was also known for promoting similar evenings in the capital for his parliamentary colleagues. In one of the Hunter's newsletters, writer Ken Hudson said there was a certain amount of cunning involved in Grahame's Wellington-based nights: 'Because it cuts down on the length of speeches in the House. You can't spout on when you've been well spiced up,' he suggested.

The original Indian curry evening at Hunter's restaurant proved so successful that Jane and Jeremy set about establishing regular theme dinners, similar to those Jane had organised many years previously at her cafe north of Wellington. Once again, Hunter's restaurant was the hub of a growing social circle in the Marlborough province.

Eventually the restaurant would return to being a lunchtime venue for diners and has recently undergone another change in style. Open during daytime hours, it has been renovated on the outside to reflect more of a New Zealand bach-like atmosphere and offers cafe-style food alongside more substantial lunchtime meals.

Chapter 16

Finesse

A wine term that describes how the delicate
flavours of the wine are in balance

Receiving acknowledgement from your peers and others is something everyone aspires to. It can come in many forms — whether it is a card to say well done on a minor achievement or a public pronouncement from a higher authority. In Jane's case the acknowledgements have been very much of the latter type and while all have been gratefully received, there has been a reticence on her behalf to publicise them.

Marlborough's regional authority publicly recognised her achievements very early on in 1988 when Hunter's won the Sunday Times Wine Club award for the third year in a row. A year later she was one of four finalists in the *More* magazine Business Woman of the Year. It was a boost to her confidence even if she didn't end up the eventual winner. Then in 1993 Jane was awarded a New Year's Honour — an OBE. When she first received the letter from Government House informing her that her name had been put forward, she was bemused as to why anyone would think she was worthy. 'I was highly embarrassed, really. I couldn't bring myself to tell anyone other than Mac about it because I thought there were lots of other people in the wine industry who deserved this more than me. Then when it got closer to being announced and I knew it was going to be in the paper, I felt really nervous. I was worried about how people would react. But it was actually quite nice because I got letters from all sorts of people congratulating me.'

On the day of the investiture Jane was allowed to have two people accompany her to Government House. She chose her sister Libby and her father. 'It was a nerve-racking experience. We were all placed into an order and then we had to file into the room where the Governor General greeted us individually, shook our hands and presented us with our medals.'

While Jane would have preferred to keep quiet about the whole thing, her distributors in the UK were doing just the opposite. The following appeared in a *Harpers* magazine article.

'In amongst the politicians and sports personalities in the year's New Year Honours list, there is an addition of a rare award in a rare category. Jane Hunter, head of Hunter's, received the O.B.E for services to the viticultural industry.

'Jane only started producing wine from her sixteen-hectare vineyard in 1983. Her English agent at the time, Andrew Hamilton, commented that not only does Jane have immense viticultural knowledge, but this is augmented by rare commercial insight. "When she took over in 1987, she realised the potential of Marlborough's cool climate for Sauvignon Blanc. It has led the New Zealand charge in Europe and won Jane more than 30 Gold Medals in local and international wine competitions." Her reputation rests on diversity and experimentation. Her Sauvignon Blanc has made her and Marlborough famous, but she made a convincing case for a wider regard in the recent Air New Zealand wine awards. Every one of her seven entries was honoured.'

There are strict regulations surrounding the use of an OBE. Jane is within her rights to add the letters after her name in all written correspondence. She doesn't always do so, although just about every letter she receives from the UK is addressed to Jane Hunter OBE.

'In countries like England, Hong Kong and India it means a lot. Even now when I do dinners and it is mentioned by someone that I have an OBE, people are keen to find out why I received it; they consider it a great honour, which of course it is. When we went to India recently some of the people were very enamoured of it. We were launching our wines along with some others from New Zealand and when we were all introduced I was announced as Mrs Jane Hunter — OBE from the Queen of England.'

She was slightly embarrassed by the reaction once people realised she had an OBE. 'All the people at my table were so terribly excited and began oohing and aahing. They kept going on about how I had been given this honour by the Queen of England. Looking back, it was very endearing. I think there is far more interest in honours like this in countries that used to be part of the Commonwealth and now aren't. They seem to love all the pomp and ceremony that surrounds anything to do with the Queen.'

The distributors in India were so impressed with her honour that they asked her if she would bring the medal with her and wear it at the official launchings. 'I couldn't quite bring myself to do that, but I did wear it for an official photo while I was there.'

While it didn't lead directly to more sales for the company, Jane admits it did help raise the profile of Hunter's wines and it has added a little romanticism to both her story and that of the company.

Following hard on the heels of her official recognition for services to the New Zealand wine industry, Jane was acknowledged in the world of science by being given an honorary doctorate by Massey University. Unbeknownst to her, officials had been considering her for some time and had been secretly interviewing not only her staff, but Jane as well. 'I was leaving the restaurant one day when this guy walked up to me and asked if I could give him some advice. He told me he was thinking of planting a vineyard and he wanted to know what he should be looking for, what clones to consider and what issues to be wary of. I must have been having a good day that day as I spent some time answering his questions. What I didn't know was he was from Massey University and he was researching me and my attitudes. That's a bit scary now when I look back on it. I'm glad I gave him some decent answers.'

Only one honorary doctorate a year is given out by Massey University, if they choose to give one at all. Having accepted the honour, Jane then had to promise to present the graduation speech to all 1000 students. 'I was getting a bit better at giving speeches by that stage so I wasn't too nervous about that part of the ceremony. I was more worried about the rigmarole I had to remember when I walked onstage to accept the degree. I knew I had to shake hands with this person, and bow to another and say something to another, while wearing all this regalia.'

In his citation on the occasion of the doctorate the University's Public Orator said the following:

'I am frankly at a loss, Mr Chancellor, whether to recommend Jane Hunter for the award of Honorary Doctorate of Commerce, in acknowledgement of her astonishing business acumen and economic perspicacity; or of an Honorary Doctorate of Letters in response to the outstanding creative imagination in all her doings; or an Honorary Doctorate of Science in recognition of her transcendent viticultural expertise. Let it be, finally, in Science since it is her understanding of the ways of the grape that has driven the rest of her achievements and it is as a viticulturist that she has captivated the imagination of New Zealand.'

Her speech to the graduates (as highlighted by Terry Dunleavy in this book's foreword) was an inspiring one and it has been remembered by many who were in the audience that day. More than ten years on, she still runs into people who were in the hall either as graduates themselves or family members of a graduate, and all comment on the impact she had.

'I find it amazing that people would even remember what I said or even that I gave the speech.'

While not demeaning the importance of the OBE or the doctorate, perhaps the greatest acknowledgement of Jane is an international award she received in 2003. Early in the year she had noticed an article promoting the upcoming inaugural Women in Wine Award. Nominations were being called for and Jane was convinced to put her name forward. It involved sending a curriculum vitae to the organisers, who then requested further information that required her to write in detail about her contribution not only to the world of wine but in other areas outside of the industry. It took some considerable time to get all the information together and once it was sent off, Jane promptly forgot about it. It wasn't until some months later when she was on her annual trip to the UK that she had cause to remember the competition. 'I had a phone call from Libby telling me that I had to be in London on such and such a date to collect an award. I didn't know what she was talking about. I couldn't figure out what award I could possibly have won. It wasn't until she mentioned the Women in Wine that I even remembered I had entered.'

The award, created by the Italian organisation Le Donne del Vino, aimed to recognise the large number of women around the world who had made significant contributions, yet might not have received the same recognition as men in similar positions. The award was to be presented as part of the International Wine and Spirits Competition in London, three weeks after Jane was notified she had won. The only problem with that was Jane was already in the UK to meet with distributors and she had to leave prior to the presentation to attend two wine dinners in Hong Kong. 'I had to leave London, fly to Hong Kong, do the dinners, fly back to New Zealand and then get straight back on a plane to London. The funniest thing about that was, because I had just met with all the distributors only a few weeks earlier, there was no work for me to do. I was told to have a holiday. You know, in all the dozens of times I have been to London over the years, I have never been in London with no work agenda filling my days. I was staying at this hotel and the first morning I woke up and thought, "Right, what do I do today?" I wandered around a bit lost for a while and then decided I would do all the touristy things that I had never had the chance to do before. I went to the Globe Theatre and St Paul's Cathedral — places I had never visited. I had a great time.'

On the night of the awards Jane was placed at the table with the president of Le Donne del Vino; looking around the room at the countries represented she felt uneasy that she had been chosen as the winner over so many other big names in the industry. 'To me it seemed weird that the award had come to someone like me from the newest wine-producing country in the world, instead of being given to someone from one of the Old World producers. But having said that, it was a huge honour, not just for me but for New Zealand as a whole.'

Of all the awards Hunter's has been presented with, this inaugural Women in Wine Award was perhaps the greatest. In Europe and America it was considered a major accolade — yet at home in New Zealand it was hardly recognised. 'Paul Holmes from Television New Zealand had pre-recorded a story with me before I flew out and that played after I had won. But hardly anyone else even covered it. We sent out a press release but the reply we got back from some of the media was "Jane Hunter and Hunter's wines have had too much publicity of late, so we won't be following up on this". How bizarre is that? What I thought New Zealand would cotton on to, was not so much that I had won, but that this was an award given for the first time by women in Italy and presented at a UK competition and in its first year you would have expected it to go to France or Italy, one of the more traditional countries, as they had been involved in winemaking for centuries. In fact, they did it the other way round because they admired what New Zealand women were doing, especially given how many fields outside of the winery women in this part of the world are involved in. They wanted to highlight that and inspire women in Europe to do similar things.'

Good friend Peta Mathias, celebrity food author and chef, believes Jane is more respected overseas than she is in her home country and this dearth of acknowledgement almost confirms that. In the UK the story ran in some papers, the BBC ran a story and later when an American author released a book on the impact of women in wine, she chose a photo of Jane to adorn the front cover. Women's organisations throughout the world were clamouring to get Jane as a guest speaker, including an organisation known as The Goddess of The Grapes, which runs annual wine dinners and tastings in Silicon Valley, California. 'The women in this organisation were all highly motivated individuals. They ran successful multi-million-dollar businesses or were members of select committees for the President. The only way they could have known about me was because of the award. I didn't get any acknowledgement at home, yet I got invited to America because of it.'

One of the areas about Jane that had impressed the judges was her involvement at the top echelons of business both within the wine industry and outside. In 1992 she had been appointed to the new HortResearch establishment board set up by the government. The board's responsibility was to bring together two established factions: one the Department of Scientific and Industrial Research, the other the Ministry of Agriculture and Fisheries, under the umbrella of the newly created Crown Research Institute. She remained a board member for four years, resigning only in 1996 when she realised she needed to be concentrating on Hunter's after the challenging 1995 vintage.

She had been a member of various local-body organisations such as the Marlborough Regional Development Board, she had been on the New Zealand Wine Institute Executive and was an inaugural member of the New Zealand Wine Guild.

During the early 1990s Jane was also commandeered by the Prime Minister, Jim Bolger, to be a member on a number of taskforces. One was an Enterprise Conference in Wellington where she, along with other business luminaries, was asked to come up with ideas to develop New Zealand industries outside of the narrow range of primary products and ensure they were internationally competitive.

Prime Minister Jim Bolger would again tap her on the shoulder a short time later, requesting her presence on Taskforce 2000. This was instigated by the government to ensure New Zealand made the most of the forthcoming Olympic Games to be held in Sydney in 2000. His brief to the small committee was to find ways of piggy-backing on the events in an effort to lure across the Tasman some of the hundreds of thousands of Games visitors set to converge on Australia.

The taskforce consisted of John Hart (who would go on to become the All Black rugby coach), David Kirk (former All Black captain), Paul Collins of Brierleys and Jane. 'Our ideas had to encompass trade, tourism and sport. One that we came up with, which you would have thought was an obvious one, was the need for a common calendar of events. With wine fairs and events we always combined it with the food industry but in other fields there was no common ground. It seemed so ridiculous that if there was a big rugby match in Christchurch, tourism operators didn't necessarily know about it. And why wasn't there an effort to establish trade exhibitions so all fields could take advantage of the tourist potential? It has become standard practice these days. If you look at the giant rugby ball in France during the 2007 Rugby World Cup, or the exhibitions held in Valencia during the America's Cup, they were joint efforts making the most of a major marketing opportunity. It is a case of pooling together to get a bigger bang for your buck.'

The taskforce worked consistently for more than two years, finally presenting their findings and suggestions to the government. But it wasn't all hard work. Jane says considering that two of the members were high-profile rugby legends, it was inevitable that she had to endure game analysis every meeting. 'The first part of every meeting was spent discussing rugby, of course. And then we had to go to a couple of games, which frankly I was horrified at. I have never quite understood rugby and to be honest I don't really like the game. But the rest of the team said we had an opportunity to make the most of the All Blacks to sell our ideas. There was this one game, New Zealand versus South Africa, and it was being played in Auckland. It was decided that it would be a good idea if we brought over some of the people from the Sydney Olympics Committee. John Hart got us this corporate box where we could watch the game and do some serious networking. I tried to get out of it and said I wasn't really needed as I didn't know a thing about rugby. No one was letting me off, though, and I was told that I did indeed need to be there. John, who was commentating on the game for television at that stage, came in just before the game and said that everyone in the box had to put up $15 and guess the correct score. The person with the closest fulltime score would get all the money. I took him aside and said, "Just one problem, John. How do you score? Do you have goals like in soccer? Or is it points like in Aussie Rules?" He was horrified. I still had to guess a score, though. So there I was sitting next to Paul Collins, and I had to keep asking him to explain what was happening. I looked away at one stage and when I turned around the players were walking off the field. I couldn't understand what was going on. Paul told me the game was over. "They don't play for very long, do they?" I said, much to his amusement. Anyway, as you probably guessed, I was the one with the correct score, so that horrified them even more. I had to shout everybody drinks for the rest of the night.'

Her ignorance of New Zealand's national game was obviously becoming a little embarrassing, so Jane decided she needed to rectify it. She signed up to become a member of the All Black Supporters' Club, much to John Hart and David Kirk's amusement. The paraphernalia she received was duly passed on to her nephews, James and Edward. But not before she had read the fine print that promised that all members of the supporters' club would be informed if any All Black player visited their town. 'I went to one of the taskforce meetings one day and said jokingly to John that I was disappointed to hear an All Black had been in Marlborough and yet I had not been informed and I never got the chance to meet him. Well, some weeks later I was in my office and one of the women from the wine shop, who was just as ignorant about rugby as I was, phoned to say there was this rather large All Black guy waiting to see me.'

The 'rather large All Black guy' turned out to be Andy Haden, a renowned former All Black who told Jane he had been talking to John Hart about travelling to Marlborough, and John had insisted that he had to go out to Hunter's winery and meet Jane. 'We had a great afternoon and it turned out that he had some knowledge of the wine industry, having brought back one of the first new clones of Merlot after a trip to France.'

She might not have had a great understanding of New Zealand's national game but Jane's knowledge of the wine industry overall was greatly admired by those in the business.

In 2003 she was asked to become a member of the board of New Zealand Wine Company, which owned Grove Mill Wines. Chairman of the board was long-time friend Mark Peters, who says Jane's attributes were a valuable asset. 'I felt we needed a woman's perspective in terms of governance and we also needed viticulture expertise. Jane had both. I have always admired her ability in all aspects of the industry and I knew that would filter through around the board table.'

Jane herself was flattered by the invitation and while some may have seen it as a conflict of interest, she disagrees. 'There were some areas where I obviously knew not to pass information on, but I have always experienced that sort of restriction. When Ernie was alive and I was working at Montana there were things I knew never to discuss. And at home my uncle was a State Liberal Party Member of Parliament, while my stepfather was a State Labour Party Member of Parliament, so I have learnt when to stay quiet. Besides, if you look at the New Zealand Wine Company and Hunter's, they are in totally different markets. They are much bigger than us, and not only do they position their wines at different price points but they also target different markets than we do. It's not about being competitive with someone like Grove Mill. The real competition doesn't come from within this region, it comes from outside. It is Marlborough against the world; we really are Marlborough Inc.'

Instead of finding the board commitments a distraction, Jane instead discovered they provided her with inspiration. 'I would have gone mad if I hadn't done that. You have to have something outside if you are in business or else you get stuck in your own little rut. Being on those boards meant I met people who were in parallel businesses and I have gained so much by being able to talk more widely and learn from others.'

Latterly Jane has been a board member of New Zealand Trade and Enterprise (NZTE), a government national economic development agency. With directives to stimulate economic growth by helping to boost export earnings, NZTE works with business both regionally and internationally. She was appointed in 2006 and Jane's experience as the managing director of an export success story has made her a popular public representative.

There have been many highlights during Jane's career, including having the chance to meet Prince Charles at Government House. 'One of the things I remember about that evening was the Prime Minister bringing the Prince around and introducing him to everybody along the way. Mr Bolger had an amazing ability to remember names, which I found fascinating. But not only that, he would introduce a person and always manage to say something about that person during the introduction. That night I was wearing a necklace that my grandmother had given me, which had these tiny little grapes on it. After he had introduced me and the people I was standing with, he started to walk away but not before he leant over to me and whispered, "Very subtle marketing, Jane", referring to my necklace.'

Adding to the special occasion, Jane was one of

only twelve individuals invited to dine with His Royal Highness. The invitation came out of the blue. 'At the cocktails this official from Government House came up to me and said, "Jane, we would like it very much if you would come through and have dinner with Prince Charles." Well, what do you say to that? Everyone else was left with their cocktails and only twelve of us went on in to dinner. There were no aides in the dining room, just the people invited. Prince Charles was hilarious. He had us in stitches telling stories about things that had happened to him during his trips round the world. I kept thinking, you poor guy. I have to do about twenty dinners a year, which can be hard. You know you are never going to meet these people again — but here he was making polite conversation with us and it was just one dinner in hundreds he must attend every year. He really was a very entertaining man. And it felt amazing to be sitting there at dinner with him. One of my highlights, I have to say.'

There were others. Meeting the Queen at Brancott in 1990, being present at the opening cocktail party for the All England Lawn Tennis Club season opening in 2004, dining with Princess Anne when she visited New Zealand, receiving a private tour of the royal ship *Britannia*, being invited to Government House for special opera performances and having morning tea and a tour of Hillsborough Castle in Belfast are just a few. But ask Jane what her greatest highlight has been and you will be surprised by her reply. 'It was being asked to present a graduation speech to my old school, St Peters Girls [Adelaide], in 2004.'

The instant response to her saying that is what on earth was so special about returning to your old school? 'Because I was the worst student ever when I was at school. Not that I caused a whole lot of trouble or anything like that, it was just I hated studying. All my reports mention how I could try harder, that I wasn't putting in enough effort, that I was lazy. And it's true. I was far from an excellent student and it's fair to say very little fired my imagination. So when I was asked to go back and speak as one of the school's success stories, it was a huge highlight.'

During her speech on the night, she spoke honestly about her reticence to succeed at school and it was quickly confirmed by people in the hall who had known her as a student. 'So many people came up to me afterwards and said things like, "You are right, you were a terrible student," which made the fact I was giving the graduation speech even more of an achievement.'

The recognition and the opportunities Jane has experienced have been a total surprise to her over the years. 'It goes on and on. I have been so lucky. In every country I have been to people have done so much for me. I kept wondering why they would go to all that effort. Sometimes I have to pinch myself, it all seems so surreal.'

It may sound rather glamorous and it would be easy to think that Jane lives life in the fast lane of movers and shakers. But in reality the highlights stand out because much of the rest of her time is spent doing the hard yards, being on the road, travelling constantly, living out of a suitcase, meeting new people all the time and having to make small talk with people she knows she will probably never meet again. But as a selling tool, Jane is vital to the company, according to Mac. 'I was unaware of how important people in the UK market regarded Hunter's when I first arrived here. I was amazed at the breadth of the wine industry as a whole over there and the competition we faced. But what surprised me the most was the reputation Hunter's had over there. And a lot of that is because of Jane. She is very important to the name — she is the flagship of the company and very important from a promotional point of view.'

David Sommerfelt, who was a director of Horseshoe Wines in the UK (one of the original distributors of Hunter's), describes Jane as a perfectionist. 'She aims for perfection and I know of no occasion when she has not succeeded. She never loses the personal touch and her workload is phenomenal.'

Jane laughs at that summary of her abilities, as she considers herself a lazy individual and found those promotional trips hard work. 'I found it very stressful. It has become easier now because I have learnt how to make small talk at these things. I never used to be able to do that. It is probably only in the last few years that I have been able to sit down and talk to people and feel comfortable. But it is still incredibly demanding. I always have to go through the business side of things when I'm away, which means I have to put myself out there. And the schedules were always incredibly tight. I would have arrived in the UK after a long-haul flight and from then on there was very little let-up, I was constantly with people. Each morning I would be picked up from the hotel and would have to travel for two or three hours, say from Devon to Cornwall. Once I arrived there were already people waiting to talk to me so I had to be ready to start talking business. Then someone would say, "Come on, Jane, it's time to get back in the car," and we would have to go somewhere else. Another two-and-a-half hours to get to wherever the dinner was that night. There was never time to change or take a rest. I'd think, "Oh well, tomorrow morning I will get up and go for a walk." But no, at quarter to eight they would be ready to head away for another day of travel and meetings. I have finally got people to realise that sort of schedule doesn't work for me. I need time out and I need time on my own, even if it is travelling alone in the back of a taxi for an hour.'

Distributor Peter Hofman, who has been involved with Hunter's since 1987, says he was well aware how taxing Jane found travel. 'There is no doubt in my mind that she found these trips very stressful. She wasn't keen on being driven around the country from one promotional tasting to another. But in spite of her reticence she was undoubtedly very effective at promoting Hunter's wines and has over the years become quite a considerable celebrity.'

A celebrity whose business attributes have been called on by the government of the day, who has been awarded an OBE for her services to the wine industry, has been given an Honorary Doctorate in Science and was the winner of the inaugural International Women in Wine Award — all before she had even reached the age of fifty.

Chapter 17

Veraison

*The time in the cycle of the grapevine
when the fruit starts to ripen*

L ife can be lonely in top management, especially if you are always on the move, travelling from one spot to another, never spending more than a few months at a time at home. The issue of always having to travel was the reason Jane sold her cob cottage in 2005 and moved to a more contained property in Blenheim. She found she didn't have the time to enjoy all the beauty she had created. The same thing could be said about her personal life. While she has had fantastic opportunities to see some of the world's greatest cities, has met with some of the world's most famous individuals and dined at renowned restaurants, it has all been done on her own.

If there is one question that is bound to be raised

whenever Jane Hunter is discussed, it is: 'Has she never remarried?' Jane herself is used to fielding the query and is perplexed at why people are so interested. She admits, though, that just as work provided her with wonderful opportunities, it also kept her from forming long-term relationships. 'I was thrown into the business and it was a huge learning curve for me. For quite a few years I didn't want to stop because I didn't want to face what had happened. I just wanted to keep going. I think the time I really had to face what had been going on was when Libby and Mac came over here — they managed to take some of the pressure off me. But then we had some difficult times and I had to keep on going. Before I knew it, time had passed on and I thought, where have all the years gone? If I had wanted to have children, it was too late. But I would never have been able to have a family and run the business as well. Also, I have always had to work with not being terribly well. I don't mean in terms of some serious illness but I do get tired very easily and I have always had to cope with really bad headaches and migraines. Whenever I go overseas I know just how much I can do and what I can't. And I know that I could never have coped with a family because whenever I get home from these trips I have to take care of myself. I wouldn't have been able to take care of a family as well.'

While there have been a number of men interested in Jane over the years it isn't until recently that she has found someone she feels totally comfortable with. 'There are always the people who wanted to know me because of who I am and my role in the wine industry, which to many people is a romantic occupation. But that isn't the reality. The reality is it is hard work and I am away from New Zealand for about a third of every year. How many men would put up with that?'

It would require a man who understood the necessities of business and the importance of Hunter's to Jane. That man is Graeme Coates, a biologist and an entrepreneurial businessman with a long history in the aquaculture industry. From 1987 until 1994 he was the director of Regal Salmon Ltd, having previously been a partner in a fish-farm consulting firm in Scotland; he is currently the principal of his own consultancy company in Marlborough and executive officer of the New Zealand Marine Farming Association. Marlborough being such a small place means the two had run across each other on numerous occasions over the years. It wasn't unusual for Hunter's restaurant to be the hub of any promotional events in the Marlborough region, where not only Jane's wines but the food of the district was showcased to visiting media. Regal Salmon, along with Riverlands Meat, Marlborough Cheese and the mussel industry, were always represented. It was after the death of Graeme's wife, Kath, in 2004 that the two met on a more social level outside of business. His attitude to life, along with his many experiences, means he is the perfect muse for Jane. 'For one thing he isn't terribly interested in the wine industry per se. He has had an incredibly interesting life and worked in some amazing places, like Scotland, India, West Africa and China, building fish farms and selling fish-farming technology. We have probably done a lot of similar things during our careers. And now we are both at that stage in life where it's nice to have someone who has common interests, to go places with. I can accompany him to the functions and I enjoy doing that. Then Graeme will come to wine functions with me and he just fits in. He is a very sociable person. He can sit down and chat away with people, and as he has done so many things in his life he quickly seems to find common ground.'

Friends of Jane claim he is the best thing to ever happen to her. Sarah Morphew Stephen says she has never seen Jane so relaxed or laugh so much. 'What's so wonderful about Graeme is that he is just as important in his own sphere and he gives her the chance to just be herself. She has always been an immensely generous person, giving of her own time, and Graeme is allowing her to indulge in that. He is a wonderful companion and there is nothing in the world like companionship. And together they laugh the whole time.'

As a former fitness enthusiast Graeme has also got Jane into the outdoors more than she thought possible, although his first efforts to encourage her to go biking nearly ended in disaster. It was an off-country bike ride along a rough gravel road. Having never used gears on a bike before, Jane was literally learning as she pedalled. From gravel to dirt, over hills and troughs, she coped admirably until the first stream crossing, which was her undoing. Crashing off the bike, she sat amidst the water and stones looking slightly dishevelled in amongst her fits of laughter. Graeme was impressed that instead of being deterred by the incident she climbed straight back onto the bike and continued on. Biking is now a regular part of her life and she has even managed to cycle across the Golden Gate Bridge in San Francisco — much to the amusement of her friends back home. 'If I had known him twenty years ago we probably wouldn't have had as much in common. Graeme was quite a sporty person and I couldn't say I was really that interested. These days he has slowed down somewhat and I guess he has developed other interests closer to many of mine. I think he has realised that he is quite a good cook recently — it's opened up a whole new world for him. I guess when you can no longer run up and down mountains or take part in ocean swimming races it's nice to know you have some other things to interest you. The two of us get on really well.'

That's as far as the very private Jane Hunter will go in terms of speaking publicly about her personal life. For Graeme there are many aspects of Jane that he admires, from her love of family through to her business skills.

But he says there is one side of her personality that most people miss. 'They see her as a strong and determined businesswoman, which she is, but they don't see the other side of her and that is her incredible generosity. I really admire that. She's not only generous with her family but also with her friends, staff and a number of charities. Time is never an issue, she will find time no matter how much pressure she is under.'

That may be why there is such loyalty among her staff, with many of the current employees having been with Hunter's for well over ten years. According to Mac, 'You have to commit murder to leave here.'

Certainly there is a tendency for winemakers to move on to bigger and brighter occupations, but in Gary's case he has stayed put since 1991 and says he is in no hurry to leave, given how much leeway Jane gives him in the winery. 'I have free range in the winemaking. If I say the Pinot Noir is not up to scratch or that much of the Sauvignon Blanc is rubbish, Jane will look at that. Having free range is a secure position to be in. That's why I have stayed — there is no board to answer to, only Jane. And she makes good decisions. Sometimes I don't agree with them but that's normal. Once she makes her decision we will head down that track.'

Having the same winemaker creating the wines for eighteen years is not only a bonus in terms of consistency, it is also a management one, according to Jane. 'Whenever we change assistant winemakers Gary has to stay close to the winery to ensure they are doing things the way he would like them done. It's very much a learning and teaching curve during that initial period. Likewise, if we had had a change in senior winemaker, I would have had to stay a lot closer to the winery and vineyards, which would have impacted on me getting out into the marketplace to sell.'

Very few companies can boast the fact that the top tier of management is still the same today as it was back in 1991. Jane says that stability has been a major marketing factor.

'It has helped us maintain our markets and to build on them. We have always had that consistency of product, despite there being vintage variation from year to year. To overcome that we open the last three year's vintages to taste and then work to ensure the quality is retained. That ensures we aren't stuck in a time warp. Also, with the three of us having worked together for so long and with Tony Jordan having been involved for more than twenty years, it means we don't have to second-guess anything. You learn the strengths and weaknesses of people over time and once you do that you can adjust your reactions accordingly. You tend to know how people are going to react. I would suggest we would be the most consistent in terms of staff, of any winery in the region.'

The long-term relationships Jane, Mac and Gary have

built up with staff and distributors are also reflected in the relationships they have back in New Zealand, particularly with growers. Hunter's has only six contract growers, all based in the renowned Wairau Valley. Some of them have been selling their grapes to Hunter's for twenty years, which is astounding given how many people chop and change in an effort to get better prices. Every year Jane sits down with her growers and individually sets the price for the upcoming season. To say it is a stressful time would be an understatement. 'It is the hardest time of the year for me. I can see it from both sides. I remember how Dad used to feel every time he had to renegotiate his grape contract as a grower, so I understand how they must feel. But then again, I have to look at it as a winery owner. On one side I know I can only afford to pay so much and on the other you have growers asking for more. I just hate it.'

She is putting herself down, according to growers who have chosen to stay with her rather than seek the more lucrative spot market. Phil Walsh has been supplying Hunter's since the days of Ernie and says while Jane is firm, she is also very honest. 'Ernie was very sharp and blunt when it came to setting prices. But Jane is extremely aware of what the market price for grapes is and she is up with the play. I am a loyal sort of person and obviously I wouldn't still be there after so many years if I felt I was being treated badly.'

David Dillon is another contract grower whose dealings with Jane go way back. His mother was one of the first growers to supply Hunter's and since her death in 2002 David has seen no reason to look elsewhere. 'Mary [his mother] held Jane in very high regard. There was no way she would ever have considered selling to anyone else. Neither would I. It feels as though we are part of the foundation of Hunter's, as we have always been able to deal with the same people all the way through. This whole grape thing can get a bit bitter and twisted but we have never had a problem. Besides, when it comes to Jane, she has that brilliant smile and that alone must be worth many noughts on the bottom of the contract. We feel privileged to be with her and I can assure you we don't take it for granted.'

It isn't always such an amicable relationship. Over the years there have been growers who have insisted they receive more for the grapes than Jane was prepared to pay. They have quickly gone by the wayside. Then there was the 1995 season when Hunter's couldn't process some of the fruit because of the poor quality. Knowing it was nothing to do with the way the growers had managed the vines, Jane offered to pay some of them regardless of the fact that she didn't bring in any of their fruit. It was an easier option than trying to salvage rotten grapes.

'Then there were others whose fruit we tried to on-sell but they wanted top prices for fruit that was way below standard. It can be a real battle, especially if you get into the situation where people are contracted but they see what the spot market is paying and want you to equal that. In a bad year such as 1995 it can be very stressful.'

Distributors, winemaker, growers, employees and vine holders have all stayed a part of the Hunter's family for years on end. Helen Neame, who runs the wine shop, has been an integral part of the business since 1994 and says newcomers to the company begin with an image of Jane that is somewhat at odds with the person she really is. 'I think a lot of people are in awe of her so they don't treat her like a real person and don't want to bother her with their problems. That can be upsetting for her. She is also very much a hands-on employer. If I am really busy in the wine shop she will come and help out — not actually in the shop itself but she will do the dishes or answer the phone. She often comes into the wine shop and potters around dusting or putting all the glasses into the dishwasher if I am dealing with visitors. How many bosses would do that?'

Being hands-on is not something people expect of Jane and she finds it intriguing that many assume she doesn't actually need to be at work every day. 'It's as if they think I sit at home and let the business run itself. If I am in the country I am at the winery every single day. Why wouldn't I be?'

The surprise when winery visitors spy Jane always

amuses Helen. 'We have people come in from all over the world and most have read about her somewhere along the line. If she happens to walk through the shop, you can see everybody start nudging each other and whispering, "That's Jane Hunter." They are in awe of her. And believe it or not, we still have people coming into the wine shop wanting to see Paddy, who died ages ago.'

The Hunter's story may be well known but Helen says tourists always want to hear the finer details. 'I would end up telling the story dozens of times a day and everyone listens in awe to it. I guess it makes us stand out from everybody else. Otherwise we are just another winery pouring Sauvignon Blanc and Pinot Noir that is very good and has won lots of gold medals. But there are other wineries out there that have done that too. I think you have to present a difference, you have to make sure people remember this winery. What Jane has achieved is what people remember about us when they leave. That and the quality of our wines.'

While she has never had children, Jane has the next best thing — two nephews who live in the same town as her. She has openly doted on them both and all her friends admit they are probably the two most important people in her life. Edward is still at college and James has just completed his degree in winemaking at Lincoln University. His decision to become a winemaker is no flash-in-the-pan one. He says ever since he was five years old he has known he wanted to be involved in the industry that has supported three generations of his family. Some of his earliest memories are of being driven through the vineyards of his grandfather, Brian Arnold, on a motorbike. He also has clear memories of the 1995 vintage, as the desperation to save some of the crops from the neverending rain permeated through to the young eight-year-old. 'I remember driving a four-wheel-drive motorbike up and down the rows picking up the bins of fruit as everyone tried to get it off before the next rainfall. There was so much rotten fruit that we couldn't do anything with, we just had to leave it on the vines or chuck it on the ground. It left quite an impression.'

James said he had no idea how the rest of the world viewed his Aunty Jane. 'When I have been overseas with Dad [Mac], I have heard all these stories about her. Especially in the UK, where you get these old guys coming up and saying how they remember Jane when she first came over in 1987 or 1988. She has obviously created quite an impression on a number of people — yet to me she's just Aunty Jane. It's quite a strange feeling. For me and my brother, she is the reason we know we can do anything we put our minds to. I often look at business people who have been really successful and think, "Wow, they must be really special to have achieved so much. I wonder what it is they know that I don't." Then I look at Aunty Jane and realise she is one of those people, she is a very clever businesswoman, but underneath it all she is just a person. She went to uni and toughed it out, she travelled, she took chances. Now look at her. She gives Edward and me the confidence to try anything.'

Having gained a considerable amount of practical experience by being able to work within the winery during his university holidays, James is fronting a new label in the Hunter's portfolio. Known as 'The Jumper', with three stick sheep on the front of the bottle, it is appealing to the younger wine-drinking generation and is already being sold in Belfast and Japan.

Jane's younger nephew Edward has still to decide on his career path — but already he is receiving a guiding hand from his aunty. His passion for music and drama has been fostered by Jane, and while she herself loves more classical music or middle-of-the-road artists, she isn't deterred by Edward and his friends' popular band that concentrates on rock music. 'She likes to encourage me and will often turn up if I am playing somewhere, even if she doesn't really like our style of music. Being in tune with James and me means she would never expect anything from us, like making us come to some business dinner or something she would know was boring to us, yet she will come to see me do things that I know she probably isn't that keen on. She is amazingly generous and I think that's partly because she loves seeing us all have a good time.'

While unsure of his future, Edward is keen to learn more about the intricacies of business, which he and Jane discuss at a very academic level. 'I would like to do business management and Aunty Jane has given me the chance to start merchandising Hunter's wines around the local supermarkets and liquor outlets. That is giving me first-hand experience of marketing — I am incredibly lucky to be able to do that. It's also been great discussing business ideas with her as she has such a sound knowledge of the marketplace.'

It's not just the local family that Jane stays in close contact with. She also travels regularly to Adelaide to catch up with her father and sister Ashley and to Italy to see her mother and stepfather. The rigours of work may have prevented her from having her own family, but it has provided her with the chance to look out for her siblings and parents, according to Libby. 'Family has always come first with her, no matter what. And Hunter's has allowed her to indulge the rest of us, which has been a great thing for her. She gets a great deal of satisfaction out of that.'

Friends are also important to Jane, Libby says, especially those friends who go back to university days. 'I think it takes a long time for people to trust others and even more so if you are someone who has become as well known as she has. She is also very shy and people tend to think she is something that she isn't, which is why her friends are people who go a long way back.'

Her closest friend is Liz Moran, who Jane went through university with. The pair have stayed in constant contact, with Jane lending a supportive ear when Liz's marriage broke up and Liz doing the same through the many ups and downs of Jane's life. 'We are a good combination as friends — I talk a lot, have ten things on my mind at once and am extremely messy, whereas Jane is quieter, speaks when there is something to say, is organised and decisive. The only area where she is indecisive would be when we are clothes shopping, but that's part of the fun. She is an incredibly supportive friend as she is always looking out for you. When I was in London in 2003, on my own for business, Jane called some of her friends over there and arranged for them to take me out. It is part of her generosity of nature that a lot of people don't see. She is still introverted but over the years she has developed excellent skills in overcoming that.'

A more recent friend is well-known chef, author and television star Peta Mathias. The two women couldn't be more different, with Peta renowned for her eccentric style of dressing and over-the-top personality and Jane being reserved and shy. The two originally met when Peta was a guest at Hunter's as part of the *Listener* Women's Book Festival. The two women hit it off and Jane was keen to have Peta back as a guest of the company in the near future. That happened a year later when Peta got her wish to star alongside poet Sam Hunt at the restaurant.

Coerced into singing Edith Piaf songs (she has a talent for singing, having trained with the famous Sister Mary Leo in Auckland), Peta told Jane she needed someone who could accompany her on piano accordion. 'Unfortunately he played with absolutely no attachment to the beat or rhythm. In the end I had to ask him to stop. Jane laughed so much she nearly cried.'

A few years later the pair took off to a renowned health resort in Queensland, sponsored by the *New Zealand Women's Weekly*. Both were expecting a week of relaxation, beautifying and gentle exercise. Peta says while some of those things were on offer, the spa wasn't exactly what they had expected. 'Somehow we had injected the word luxury into the equation, a fantasy that never eventuated.'

Instead, it saw them detoxing for two days, and Jane says that if she had eaten one more piece of broccoli she would have started turning green. Then there were the wake-up calls at 5.30 each morning to ensure they made it to the t'ai chi classes. Yoga and meditation followed plus some strenuous exercise regimes that had the women puffing and panting. 'In our little hut there was this fridge and absolutely no gin and tonic, much to Peta's disgust. All we had was a jug of iced water and six green tea bags. But by the end of the day we couldn't even face the green tea bag, we were so exhausted. We literally fell into bed every night. It wasn't what we had expected but it was a great week. And we laughed the whole time.'

Peta admits many people are surprised when they hear of her friendship with Jane. 'Even though we seem very different and you wouldn't think we would be friends, we somehow found each other interesting. You don't get to know Jane easily but she inspires great devotion from people who do get close to her.'

That devotion has been shown by many individuals who have worked alongside Jane, either within the wine industry or on the many boards she has been involved in. It has also led to opportunities for the business itself. David Kirk, who had been on the Taskforce 2000 project, realised Jane had an interest in playing tennis. He suggested to her that she phone one of his father's friends in London next time she was over there.

'He said if I ever wanted a game while in London I should call this guy because he worked at Wimbledon. I used to think, you don't just ring someone up and go and have a game of tennis at Wimbledon. What on earth is David talking about? I did actually meet this friend, John McDonald, and he used to say the same thing. I couldn't understand why people would keep suggesting I play at Wimbledon — I was only a social player, not a tennis expert. What I didn't realise was that outside of the Wimbledon competition the club is just a normal tennis club, the All England Lawn and Tennis and Croquet Club. I felt rather silly when I finally realised what they were going on about.'

Hunter's are now on the wine list of the Club Members' Private Dining Room, alongside some of the world's most renowned wine labels. Jane's many friends based in London have always looked out for her on her frequent trips to that part of the world. On the occasion of her fiftieth birthday, John and Peter Hofman insisted on taking her to one of the top restaurants in London, Langan's Brasserie, for lunch. While awaiting her first course Jane was certain she recognised one of the restaurant's other guests. 'I turned to John and said, "Is that Barry Gibb?" Now you have to realise that I am a huge Bee Gees fan and there was Barry and various other members of the Gibb family in the same restaurant as me. I was so excited and John obviously realised that. He called the sommelier over and asked me if I had a business card on me. I handed one over and he asked the waiter to deliver a bottle of Hunter's Pinot Noir, which Langan's had on their wine list, to the private room where the Gibb family was eating. Next thing you know I turned around and there was Barry Gibb standing beside me at the table. He had come out to personally thank me for the wine. Apparently, they had all just been to Buckingham Palace to receive their CBEs from the Queen. Meeting him was the best fiftieth birthday present I could have wished for.'

Through work Jane has visited dozens of different countries, but in 2001, on holiday with friend Karen Rose, she had the opportunity to visit Vietnam for the first time. It opened up a whole new world for her and she has since revisited the country four times. If there was ever somewhere she felt she wanted to give something back to, Vietnam is it — for a variety of reasons. 'The people are fascinating, so calm and yet so energised, if that makes sense. They are very accepting about what has happened to them and what they have to do to get on. But there is a huge need for support over there as the government is broke and they can't afford to do things for the people. Of all the places I have been to, Vietnam is somewhere I keep wanting to go back to. I would like to be able to put some money into a school or project over there. I have been trying to find the best way of doing it.'

Her philanthropy is something you are unlikely to hear Jane discussing. But speak to those who know her well and you quickly discover she has been an ongoing sponsor of guide dogs in training, has sponsored children overseas and given to numerous other charities within her own community and outside of it. Sharing her good fortune is part of her nature and, just like in every other aspect of her life, it is one she keeps very private.

Chapter 18

Mature

*A wine term that indicates the wine
has aged to its potential*

Innovation has been the hallmark of Hunter's ever since the first wines burst onto the New Zealand scene in 1982. It was one of the very first boutique wineries to be established in Marlborough, with mail order, newsletter and wine shop. There was the 'buy a vine' project, the on-site restaurant and the winning of international accolades. While Ernie had always been touted as being a master marketer, Jane deserves equal admiration for her abilities. The innovative schemes didn't end just because Ernie was no longer on the scene. On the contrary, Jane continued with many of his ideas and added a few of her own.

Her decision to sell wine in supermarkets and provide tastings for the shopping public was an innovative promotional tool, especially considering how dramatically the market was changing. She has instigated new products, Maori names for her wines and marketing tools. She has also continued to front up personally at wine dinners held here in New Zealand and overseas. 'People often ask why we still bother doing these dinners. But my philosophy is you have to get people to taste the wine before they will consider buying it. Ours isn't the dearest Sauvignon Blanc in New Zealand but it is one of the medium-priced ones. If we want people to buy it and it's more expensive than the wines on promotion at the supermarket, they need to have tasted it and know there is a difference.'

Her ability to size up a promotional opportunity is well known. She can instantly determine whether or not it is advantageous for Hunter's Wines overall. In the 1990s she was often the major sponsor of musical events, teaming up with Stewart MacPherson to help promote *Blood Brothers*, *Chess* and Russell Watson as they toured New Zealand. Careful to always ensure she linked the company name with quality events, Stewart says she knew that such tours were a valuable marketing tool. 'She was quick to agree to be a part of the shows because she knew it would tie in beautifully with the quality and integrity of the performance.'

Her major sponsorship in recent years has been Marlborough's popular garden show. The event began on a small scale with the goal of promoting the region's perfect climate and array of private gardens. Initially run over three days, it attracted hundreds of people to Marlborough to take part in guided garden tours that covered every possible scenario, from courtyard gardens to large country affairs set in amongst the harsh conditions of the east coast. Guest speakers from around the world held workshops on a wide range of issues, while arts and crafts and all forms of gardening paraphernalia were on display at a garden fete held in the centre of Blenheim. Even though the event hadn't been running for many years, it was obviously a highly successful formula that attracted people from throughout New Zealand. Accepting the offer of the naming rights wasn't something Jane had to think long and hard about. 'I said yes straight away. It was an excellent event and it covered everything good about Marlborough. I often say that there is more to this region than just wine. And Hunter's Garden Marlborough is an event that shows just that. The people who are visiting get to go out in the Marlborough Sounds waterways and visit back-country gardens; they are eating in our restaurants and they go shopping. It's a real showcase of everything good this region has to offer. There is a great synergy between the event itself and Hunter's and I'm really proud to be associated with it.'

Hunter's Garden Marlborough is now one of the largest events on the local calendar and has been extended to cover five days. Thousands of people take part in the tours and workshops, while millions of dollars are pumped into the local economy.

Jane also appreciated early on that visitors to the cellar door needed more than just a sample of wine to inspire them. When local artist Clarry Neame approached her asking if there was any chance of getting a studio on site, Jane began scouting for possible solutions. 'I could see that it would be a great idea but we just didn't have any spare room at that stage. It was some time later that Jeremy Jones rang me to say he had found a hut for sale that would make a perfect studio. We had it moved to the winery and Clarry has been with us ever since. It's wonderful for visitors to be able to come to the wine shop and then stop off and visit Clarry or just watch him paint. It's worked really well.'

Clarry is now a major force within New Zealand's art world, with many of his works adorning galleries throughout the country. The success of his residency at the winery was noticed by other industry members and within a few years there were a number of wineries promoting local artists, either by displaying their works or providing space for them to paint on a full-time basis.

Despite all of her successes, though, Jane is still reluctant to call herself an innovative businesswoman. 'No, I am a viticulturist. Even now I would rather be out walking the vineyards but I haven't done that seriously for some years, as it's now Bryan Vickery's responsibility as viticulturist to do that for me and it would be undermining him if all of a sudden I started getting out there, telling him how to do his job. It just wouldn't work. Besides, I am probably so out of touch now I wouldn't know what I was doing.'

Her lack of faith in her ability as a businesswoman climaxed in 2003, when New Zealand's wine industry struck tough times. 'We had got to a point where Gary, Mac and I had been doing the same job for a number of years. I didn't believe I was the right person to be running Hunter's at that stage. Even now I still think of getting in a senior marketer or CEO, as I tend to think I am not doing a good enough job. I decided we needed to have a board that would make us think about things differently and provide us with some structure that we didn't have.'

Hunter's were not in isolation regarding the problems they were dealing with. They were industry-wide issues. Number one was the failure of the American market to live up to expectations. There had been a natural expectation the States would follow on from the successes of the UK. In reality it wasn't to be. The USA was very different from the UK. Wine wasn't the average consumer's drink of choice. Every state seemed to have a different approach to sales and companies required a range of distributors to ensure a spread throughout the vast country. The fluctuating value of the New Zealand dollar meant exporters were at the mercy of the money market and to top it off consumers in America weren't as aware of Sauvignon Blanc as their British counterparts were, according to Jane. 'Sauvignon Blanc is not seen as a top-quality variety over there, probably because it isn't grown in great quantities in the States. And the price of it was very difficult for all of us. We would have liked to see our wine sitting around the US$18 mark. But in reality it was sitting at $16 or even $15, which meant we had to squeeze margins just to get a foothold.'

Secondly, the New Zealand domestic market wasn't much brighter. The impact of supermarket sales really began to kick in at the beginning of the 2000s. Prices and margins were being squeezed down as the grocery chains used wine as a loss leader in an effort to increase market share.

Thirdly, prices for grapes and overall infrastructure were constantly rising.

For smaller mid-sized wineries like Hunter's, all the issues were influencing profitability. Jane honestly believed a board of governors could provide the answer or at least help provide some solutions.

Looking back, Jane admits she could have achieved more if she had taken on consultants in varying fields, particularly someone with experience in business analysis. 'I had been saying for years that I didn't think we had a good enough understanding of what everything was costing us. It wasn't so obvious when we were in the allocation phase and selling everything we produced with good margins, but as things got tougher for us we needed to take a close look at and try to understand the margins and cost analysis. It became vitally important. This industry is no longer a lifestyle and it is no longer a business where if you win a gold medal or a trophy you can go out and publicise it to help sell the wine. That may have worked for us back in the eighties and nineties but it doesn't work that way now.'

Her fear of not understanding all the nuts and bolts of the business led her to employ Greg McCarthy, a corporate and strategic adviser from Wellington, to provide an overview of the company. She says his involvement saved them from certain disaster.

'If we hadn't done that we probably wouldn't be here today. That's how bad it had got. We needed to understand the cost of everything, right down to the last little thing. We needed to gain an understanding of how far down we could go in our pricing of each product in all of our markets, especially when selling to supermarkets. That area is so price driven, meaning we have to know exactly what every bottle of wine is costing us to produce before we can begin to agree to discount.'

Greg says it's obvious that the industry has undergone some dramatic changes in recent years.

'Historically the wine industry has been an industry where the margins have been big enough to allow for things going wrong. People could still make money even if they didn't get everything right. Whereas now you can't afford to get things wrong, the margin just isn't there. In the last ten years, the cost of grapes has gone up every year, but the price of wine has either come down or stagnated. There isn't one product line that this business makes today that it gets more money for than it did five years ago.'

It is an industry, he says, where size actually does matter. 'Previously you could have been a 10,000 up to 20,000 case winery and done okay. You could have lived at a comfortable level, but I don't think you can do that now. I believe the minimum you can live at comfortably now is 50,000 cases and probably even higher, up to 100,000. If you aren't at that number then you will have to grow steadily. So we have geared the business to reaching its physical capacity, which is 80,000 cases, and are looking at extending it further.'

Greg pointed out to Jane that there were wines the company was making that weren't returning any money; they have now been dropped from the portfolio. Sales staff were laid off and Hunter's developed a relationship with a new national distributor, which has seen a marked increase in domestic sales. He also advised her to look at the pricing structure of the wines. 'Margins have changed dramatically over the years because of the proliferation of wineries. If, say, someone comes in and has got much bigger volumes than we have and they want to sell it at $9.99 a bottle, where does that leave us who want to sell our wine at $18.99? In the earlier days, when there were more independent retailers, you could get away with staying at that price point because the retailer would hand sell your wine, knowing the quality equalled the price. The growth of supermarket sales has changed all that.'

Insecurity is an insidious thing. It starts to take over, planting doubts where previously there were certainties. Jane admits she was confused about where Hunter's was going. 'We sat down and thought about whether we might be better off to shrink in size and decrease our production. That may sound silly but we did seriously consider it when we were struggling. But after thinking about it for a while we realised it wouldn't work. We would have had to cut staff and that would have meant Gary, Mac and I would need to be much more hands on. I'm not sure any of us wanted to do that. We had already experienced that level of workload and we knew what a huge commitment that was. I for one couldn't imagine going back to that.'

There were other alternatives — Jane could have sold the company or taken on shareholders. She has vehemently resisted doing either. Many individuals have offered to help list Hunter's on the share market but Jane wasn't keen to have to answer to shareholders whose needs would be very different from the needs of the winery and probably herself. But she did consider and discuss with her advisers the benefits of taking on a partner. One of the advantages would have been greater access to formal international marketing expertise, but the downside would have been a level of restriction the company was not used to. Could the company retain its quality creed if someone else was helping pay the bills? That left the option of selling outright. It's something Jane has been threatening to do since she took Hunter's over in 1987. 'I used to ring Tony Jordan every six weeks or so and say, "I've had enough, I just can't bear it." Something would have gone wrong and I'd tell him that I was going to put the For Sale sign out front. He'd always be calm and say, "Look, what's the problem?" We'd talk it through and he'd come up with some solutions. Then everything would be all right for six weeks or so and then something else would happen and I'd be back on the phone to him again telling him I had had enough and was selling up.'

In reality, though, Jane is a focused fighter and very determined. 'When things are going bad, that's the time I want to stick in there because I have to get it back to the height it was. And then when it gets up there, it's quite easy for a while so I relax and am happy with everything — until we go down again.'

Close friend James Hatfield believes there is another, more simplistic reason why Jane hasn't sold. 'A lot of the business success of Jane and Hunter's came out of how much she missed Ernie. To let it go would have been to say a final goodbye to him and I don't think she ever wanted to do that.'

That's not to say Hunter's hasn't been targeted, says Jane. 'We have had approaches over the years to be bought out or to merge. I guess I have a very conservative approach and I have held it back somewhat. I didn't want it to get bigger. It's hard for a small winery these days but it can't be any easier for the larger ones. They just have a different set of problems that are hard to overcome. Would I sell? Probably not. I guess you have to some day but we will wait and see what happens with the next generation of people coming on.'

She is referring to her nephews Edward and James. Both have attributes that may see them following in their aunty's footsteps, with Edward showing interest in the business side of the company and James in the winemaking. While still completing his winemaking degree, James often assisted his father on Hunter's marketing trips overseas. Jane knows from experience that you cannot run a company in isolation. 'Hunter's is not just Jane Hunter. I learnt that when Ernie died. If you don't have a physical back-up team, people wonder what will happen in the long run. Which is why we have introduced James along the way, so people realise there is someone else coming along. I appreciate that you need to have young people on your team if you want to grow. When Mac and James were in Dublin and Belfast it was James that went out with all the sales guys. We — Mac, Gary and I — are considered the old fuddy duddies and while the distributors may be our age, the people who are out there selling the wine are so much younger, so I consciously utilise all the younger members of the staff, including James. And it is working in terms of sales, in a round-about way.'

Given that her nephew has always known he would end up in the wine industry, James is under no obligation to work at Hunter's. In fact, he says he will be 'banished' now he is a fully fledged winemaker. 'It has always been understood that I would go away. Both Aunty Jane and my parents have made sure that I have travelled and that I know what is out there. There are a lot of things that I want to do before I am ready to come back to Blenheim — if I decide to come back. I can't learn everything here, I need to go away. Pinot Noir is my passion and I want to go to every Pinot-producing place in the world. So I will be away for a while, maybe forever, who knows.'

Jane, in turn, has never placed any pressure on either James or Edward to become a part of Hunter's. 'What I have said to both the boys is if you want to become involved in the industry then do it, but never think that you have to come back to Hunter's. Both boys have to want to come back here for themselves — not for me or their parents. And who knows, someone may come along with an offer I can't refuse and then it won't be here for them to come back to.'

If either nephew was to come back to the winery in the next few years, don't expect Jane to be racing off into retirement. 'God no! What on earth would I do then? I mean, look at my job. I get to travel round the world, visiting some of the greatest countries and eating in some of the world's best restaurants. They are all things people would love to be able to do during their retirement years. Yet I am doing them while I work. The great thing about this job is that I don't have to retire at fifty-five, or sixty-five, or even seventy-five. So long as I am enjoying it, why on earth would I want to leave it?'

Those close to her also don't believe she will be handing the reins over any time soon. Her sister Libby says Jane couldn't survive without the winery. 'She thrives on it, even though being so shy it has been hard for her. But I don't think she would live happily without it. She will be there forever I think, in one way or another, she couldn't not be.'

Her younger sister Ashley also can't see Jane walking away, although at times she wishes she would. 'I think it's lovely to come home to your roots. There is nothing like the place where you grew up, even if it has changed over the years. Jane has very strong connections to this part of the world and it would be lovely for her to be able to come back to it. I just hope she does give herself that reward at the end — whenever that might be.'

After more than twenty-five years as a member of Marlborough's wine industry Jane is regarded by many as the matriarch, a title she is probably horrified by. She has a number of attributes that have helped keep her at the helm of Hunter's, not the least being determination. But for Mac, who has worked alongside her since 1991, her ability to remain interested is her greatest quality. 'I think it is a real feat to still have an enthusiasm for the business and want to continue it. Jane has that. The region grows good grapes and you can make good wine here, but while it's becoming more competitive all the time, the enthusiasm to keep going is a real achievement.'

Chapter 19

Cellaring

*The laying down of wines in optimum conditions
to allow their full promise to be achieved*

The earliest pioneers of the modern wine industry were quick to realise that Marlborough, while it may be small in size, was huge in terroir. It is an oft-used term that has many wine industry personnel cringing — but when it comes to describing just why one region is a world beater at producing great wines, there is no other word that says so much. How else do you describe the synergy between soil conditions and climate so succinctly?

Sip a mouthful of Marlborough Sauvignon Blanc and you will instantly recognise the explosion of fruit flavours. It is intense, zesty, zingy and totally unique. It has taken less than thirty years to go from an unknown quantity to a world-revered style of wine, taking the Marlborough region along with it. But Sauvignon Blanc, while it is the most important variety grown in Marlborough, is not a standalone entity. It may make up more than 60 per cent of all the plantings in the province, but there is plenty more for winemakers to get excited about. Pinot Noir is the second arm of the industry, both as a table wine and as a base for sparkling wines. Very fragrant wines with refreshing texture, the Pinot Noirs are quickly gaining a name for themselves. Chardonnay in Marlborough is crisp and again zingier than those produced in warmer regions. Then there are the aromatics — Riesling, Gewürztraminer and, more recently, Pinot Gris — all turning heads the world over.

The growth of Marlborough has been nothing short of phenomenal. When Hunter's first began there were only four other wineries based in the area. Only one of those had a cellar door. Compare that with the figures in 2007 — 104 wineries were registered in Marlborough and more than forty of them operated cellar doors. Likewise, the number of individuals growing grapes in 1983 was less than eighty; in 2007 there were 530.

In recent years new areas have opened up within the boundaries of Marlborough. Whereas all the first grapes were planted around the Wairau Plains, there has been a subtle shift into outlying valleys, and sub-regionality is becoming a popular byword. Marlborough has become a tourist destination with thousands of visitors a year making their way here to taste first hand the wines of the region at their source. A Wine Research Centre has been established and is now the hub of all scientific research into grape growing and winemaking in New Zealand. Nelson Marlborough Institute of Technology offers winemaking courses and many companies in the region take on apprentices in both viticulture and oenology. Foreigners flock to the region every year to take part in vintage, all keen to learn more about why Marlborough wines are so unique.

There has also been a marked change in the structure of the wine industry. While Montana founded it originally, it was the boutique wineries that gave the region its character. Many of those have now merged with larger companies and consolidation is an ongoing reality. Even the bigger players haven't been immune. In 2000 one of the original Marlborough believers, Corbans Wines, was taken over by Montana. Within a few years Montana themselves were the subject of a takeover bid when British-based Allied Domecq bought 95 per cent of the company's shares. Allied Domecq would later be sold to Pernod Ricard. In 2001 Ponder Estate was sold to Berringer Blass Wines Estate, part of the Fosters Group. Wither Hills was bought by Lion Nathan, and Nobilos bought Selaks and in turn were gobbled up by Constellation Wines. It's hard to keep track of who owns what these days, according to Jane. 'There has been a real change since 2000, with such buy-in by corporates. On top of that there has been an onslaught of grower labels appearing in the market, which has made it terribly competitive for all of us. When I arrived here in 1983 there was only a smattering of vines. There is no way I could have predicted the industry would grow so much in such a short time. Even back in 2000 there was no indication it would get as big as it is now. Hindsight is such a great thing, isn't it? I now wish I had bought more land earlier on. It is one of my regrets that I didn't, as it would have given me more control of the company's destiny in terms of cropping levels, grape prices and the associated overheads. But all the advisers I have had over the years have said, "Don't buy vineyards yet, they will come down in price. Grape prices will come down as well." In reality, the prices have continued to go up. I have managed to snatch up a couple of vineyards over the years, but in hindsight we should have bought heaps more. But then we didn't know how much this region was going to grow.'

Mac is another who was waiting for, in fact expecting, the prices to drop. 'I was one who said this industry is just like every other in the agricultural sector, there will be a cycle of boom and bust and we had to be prepared for both. We have always taken that rather conservative view, probably to our cost, especially when it came to buying more land. We couldn't see forward enough that land prices would continue to rise. They keep going up and up. Over the years we have talked with Tony and all of us have agreed that those prices can't keep on rising — but so far they have.'

While she may bemoan the fact she didn't have the foresight to buy up in years gone by, Jane does own four vineyards — which is four more than she inherited back in 1987. She leases another three and these, along with her six contract growers, are helping to increase production, which in turn is placing pressure on the marketing ability of both Jane and Mac. 'We have to be constantly on the lookout for new markets, we can't afford to sit back and expect the ones we have already established to take up the increase.'

While the UK is a vital market and always will be, there are others where Hunter's wines are equally sought after. Hong Kong is an important market for the company, even though sales aren't anywhere near the level of the UK. It is a fortuitous market in many ways, one that eventuated after Hunter's won a national award. The Tradenz Air New Zealand Export Excellence Award for a Regional Exporter was presented to Hunter's in 1993, recognising the export growth of the company in the previous twelve months. In that period of time, Hunter's overseas sales rose by 61.8 per cent by volume, with foreign exchange earnings as a percentage of total sales rising by more than 13 per cent.

'It was a great validation of what we were doing, especially for me. This was an award that was judged by a business group and it dealt with turnover, export earnings and business plans. It was more related to what I had achieved, rather than what the wine had achieved. There again, if I am honest, that was the best year ever to be judged on, as we had had a hiccup with our distributors in the UK and the States, so our export sales had been very low. We had to divert a lot into the domestic market prior to 1993. Once we did that, we appointed new distributors in both overseas markets, which ensured our sales in the twelve months prior to the awards were well up compared with previous years. It was just one of those freak times when the figures looked exceptionally good.'

Receiving a trophy wasn't the only bonus of winning the award; there was also the prize of a trip to Hong Kong or Seoul, with New Zealand Tradenz back-up to establish a distribution network. 'We had been selling wine into Singapore for some time but we hadn't thought about expanding into the rest of Asia. Now Hong Kong is by far our biggest Asian market. It would probably be our highest-profile market too, after the UK.'

European markets, including Denmark and Switzerland, whilst still small, are increasing steadily, as is the country of Jane's forebears — Sweden. 'We have always sold into Ireland, Ernie's homeland, but to me there is a great deal of satisfaction about getting our wine into Sweden, as that's where my father's family came from and it's a difficult market to crack.'

Despite the management team of Hunter's all being Australian, Jane says breaking into the Aussie market has been difficult. That is changing now with a recent upsurge in sales, as Marlborough Sauvignon Blanc has captured the consumers' palates. Other more exotic countries are beginning to open up as well, which in many ways has a lot to do with the consolidation of Marlborough as a wine-producing region. 'In the last couple of years we have had new overseas distributors come to us looking specifically for a family-owned winery to represent. They want to build a rapport rather than work with another corporate or with a nameless person who will move on with the next takeover.'

A Russian supermarket chain was one party that made an approach requesting product. Then in 2007 United Breweries (UB) in India sought Hunter's wines out for distribution. UB is India's largest liquor distributor, with India itself deemed one of the fastest-growing markets in the world. Paralleling the development of its IT industries, there is an emerging layer of wealth materialising in India, which is where UB is directing its sales. While UB could have sought out any number of New Zealand wine producers, they were adamant they wanted to deal only with private, family-owned companies. Jane knows the market is tiny at this stage, but believes that within five to ten years, India could grow to be a major export market for Hunter's.

Jane has discovered in recent years that being privately owned is an important selling point, and not only in new markets. One of her long-term marketing advisers, Wayne Ormondy, had been encouraging her to personalise her wines by placing Jane Hunter on the label. She resisted for years. It had been hard enough to be the marketing face of the company, dealing one on one with agents, markets and consumers. There was no way she wanted to get any more personal than that. But she couldn't hold out forever. 'In the end, Wayne convinced me that it was a sensible marketing move. He kept saying one of the greatest strengths we had in the market was we still had a face and were owned by an individual. We weren't a corporate wine company and we needed to promote that. He would have liked to change the label so it read Jane Hunter's Marlborough Sauvignon Blanc, but I was dead against it being that bold. I had learnt very early on that if too much emphasis is placed on one person then you risk losing market share when that person is no longer involved. So we settled for a more subtle Jane Hunter signature on the label and I insisted we have a gap between my name and the Hunter's brand name. I also wanted the winemaker's name on the label so it wasn't just me dominating the image. It has worked well and in reality if we had done it twenty years ago when it was first suggested to me, it might have made a difference to our sales.'

As the first decade of the new century draws to a close, Jane and other wine producers in Marlborough have a number of issues to deal with if the industry is to continue to grow. Finding a market to sell your product is just one small part of the equation. Perhaps the biggest part is the cost of that product, and that is an area of great concern to the entire industry. As Greg McCarthy points out, there isn't one product Hunter's made in 2008 that was making more money than the same product in 2003. Continued prise rises, from grapes through to fuel, power and wages, combined with high interest rates and the value of the New Zealand dollar, are putting the squeeze on all wine companies. Ironically, they are the same issues Ernie faced back in 1985. 'The crunch came back then and very nearly killed the wine industry and I think it is happening again now. We cannot go on absorbing all these price increases without being able to recoup them at the other end. Eventually something has got to give, otherwise a lot of people are going to end up out of business. There is bound to be more consolidation, probably in the smaller to mid-sized wineries. That's not necessarily a bad thing — but it would be tragic if we were to lose our unique family operations that have helped establish the New Zealand and Marlborough wine name.'

The pioneers of the Marlborough wine industry worried about securing markets, having to deal with consumer fickleness, high interest rates, a perceived lack of government support and taxes that seemed punitive. Leading into the 2008 General Election, the chairman of the board of New Zealand Winegrowers, Stuart Smith, said that many of those issues raised in the 1980s were still on the agenda. Excise tax and its impact on small companies was one issue of contention, as was the impact of the high New Zealand dollar.

Marlborough is a very different place to the one Jane first encountered in 1983. The change in landscape is perhaps the most obvious. 'When I first flew into Marlborough it was the middle of summer and looking down all I could see were parched fields from one end of the valley to the other. Now when you fly in it is a sea of green, even in a drought year. The province's infrastructure has also changed dramatically. Marlborough is now far more cosmopolitan than when I arrived. There are cafes and bars, restaurants and lodges. Whereas once you would only have ever heard the English language, now you hear French, Italian, Thai and German. People actually want to visit and stay here in Marlborough, not just pass through on their way to some other destination. Some may think we have become a monoculture, based solely on the wine industry — that may be true of the landscape, but the wine industry has also allowed the rest of Marlborough to grow alongside of it. There is something else the wine industry has done for Marlborough and that is to provide a range of opportunities for the next generation. We had a small community where all the children used to have to leave to find careers. Now the second generation are coming through and there are many aspects of winemaking, viticulture and hospitality that are attracting those younger people back. Just look around the region and you will see so many wineries where the founder's children are working alongside them. There is a whole new generation that is becoming part of the Marlborough legacy.'

In the thirty-five years since the first grapes were planted in Marlborough, the region has gone from being unknown to a world leader. There have been numerous ups and downs, successes and failures, but as Jane once quoted to students at her former school: 'Life is not about what happens to you — it's about what you do with what happens to you.'

'I always say I have been very lucky, but I was once told there is no such thing as luck in business. There are opportunities, and life is about how you manage and deal with the opportunities, that come your way. Is it luck that has seen Marlborough Sauvignon Blanc become a world leader? Or is it the hard work that so many individuals have put into developing this style of wine? It would be easy for the industry to rest on its laurels but we can't afford to do that. There is no doubt that there will be more challenges, but Hunter's is in a good position and I am quietly confident of Marlborough's future.'

Epilogue

There is no dog falling over himself to greet you when you arrive at Jane's home. Instead, there is a sense of calm and order, as classical music wafts from the stereo. Photos of friends, family and canine companions adorn every available space, a constant reminder of what is important in her life. There is also very little left of the shy woman who opened her door to face two policemen back in 1987. The eyes are the same startling blue, the smile still hovers at the edges and the determined stance is apparent. But the insecurities, the fear of the unknown and the sense of walking in someone else's shadow have disappeared.

The Jane Hunter of today is a very different Jane Hunter from the one who struggled to come to terms with her husband's loss. In her place is a confident and secure woman who lately has found companionship for the first time in twenty years. This is a woman who is assured enough to stride onstage and present a speech to hundreds of people, without getting a migraine or becoming ill with nerves. She can fly halfway round the world to host a wine dinner on behalf of her agents without getting violently sick. She isn't daunted having to sell Hunter's wines to distributors, something she never believed she would be able to do. 'I used to say that when Ernie died, he left me with a business that wasn't doing so well, a bloody great dog, a goat and a derelict cottage.'

No one, especially not Jane, could have imagined how she would turn that around.

There are very few regrets — although as she gets older she misses her family more. 'If there was a regret, it is being away from my family. That sounds ridiculous I know, but the fact is that when you establish a business somewhere like this, it becomes very hard to just walk away from it. As I get older I want to spend more time with my family and friends. Whilst Adelaide isn't far away, it is difficult to get to. I am very aware that because of Hunter's the family is split. Half of us are over here, Libby and I, and Dad and Ashley are back in Australia. Then Mum's in Italy. I feel very aware of that and the fact it is because of me.

'In terms of business regrets, I think we should have made much more of the awards that we earned. But our own modesty prevented us from doing that. I guess we should have also followed Bill Floyd and Wayne Ormondy's suggestion to capitalise on the Jane Hunter image a lot earlier than we did. But hindsight is a great thing.'

Walking the vines, being able to kick the dirt, pull a few leaves and taste the fruit are now distant memories. Sure she can still go and do all those things if she wants — but these days it is harder to find the time away from the desk or travel to immerse herself in the growing side of the wine.

'As the business has grown, so too has my need to be a manager. I don't get the opportunity to do the things that attracted me to the job in the first place. It's a sad reality that the aspects of the job that I loved, the reason I chose this career, those jobs are being done by others — not me. I guess that's when the crunch comes, when I have to decide, do I keep on doing this or do I get someone in to do the management job so I can get back to doing what I originally loved? I don't know the answer to that one. I do believe, though, that I have been very privileged to be a part of the Marlborough success story and to be a part of living history. I was here in the early days and I have watched this region and this industry grow. How many people get the chance to be a part of something like that, to be a part of an industry that goes from nothing to being a world leader? Hunter's is a small company in a very small country, but to go into some of the world's top restaurants and see our wines included on their wine lists is humbling. I have no doubt there are challenges ahead for all of us — but that is life. We have to make the most of those challenges, just as we have done for the past thirty years.'

A quick perusal of the photos surrounding Jane in her home doesn't shed light on any of what could be called her major achievements. There is no photo of her meeting the Queen, nothing of her with her OBE, no photo of her receiving her Honorary Doctorate or the Women in Wine Award. That's not to say she doesn't think these are important. But in the scheme of things, the photo of James as a toddler pulling the cork out of a bottle of Hunter's wine has far more meaning, as does the photo of Edward curled up on a couch with Paddy.

Who would have guessed, back in those dark days following Ernie's death, that Hunter's would still be operational more than twenty years later? Who would have contemplated that Hunter's would be the only Marl-borough company established in the early 1980s to still be owned by its original family more than twenty-five years after being founded? Who could have foreseen the growth of the region as a whole? And who could have predicted that the shy young viticulturist, who hated flying, meeting people and had never sold a bottle of wine in her life, would go on to become one of New Zealand's iconic wine industry figures?

While she may not have given birth to it, Jane Hunter is the one responsible for growing a legacy.

Appendix

Hunter's Trophies and Awards 1982–2008

1982

SILVER MEDALS

Marlborough Müller Thurgau Dry — New Zealand National Wine Show

Canterbury Grey Riesling — New Zealand National Wine Show

Pinot Gris — New Zealand National Wine Show

1983

SILVER MEDALS

Marlborough Müller Thurgau Dry — New Zealand Easter Show

Canterbury Gewürztraminer Medium — New Zealand Easter Show

Canterbury Grey Riesling — New Zealand Easter Show

Chauce Gris — New Zealand Easter Show

1984

SILVER MEDALS

Chauce Gris 1982 — New Zealand Easter Show

Müller Thurgau Dry 1984 — New Zealand National Wine Competition

Müller Thurgau Dry 1982 — New Zealand National Wine Competition

Chauce Gris 1982 — New Zealand National Wine Competition

Traminer Riesling 1984 — New Zealand National Wine Competition

1985

Sauvignon Blanc 1984 — Trophy Highest Points South Island Winemaker, New Zealand Easter Show

1986

Chardonnay 1985 — Export Trophy, Air New Zealand Wine Show

Gewürztraminer 1986 — Hospitality Trophy, Air New Zealand Wine Awards

GOLD MEDALS

Chardonnay 1985 — International Wine and Spirit Competition UK

Chardonnay 1986 — Sunday Times Vintage Festival UK

Chardonnay 1986 — Australian Royal National Wine Show

Rhine Riesling 1986 — Air New Zealand Wine Awards

Gewürztraminer 1986 — Air New Zealand Wine Awards

Sauvignon Blanc 1985 — International Wine and Spirit Competition UK

Sauvignon Blanc 1986 — Air New Zealand Wine Awards

Sauvignon Blanc 1986 — Australian Royal National
Wine Show

Sauvignon Blanc 1986 — Sunday Times Vintage
Festival UK

Fumé Blanc 1985 — Sunday Times Vintage Festival UK

1987

GOLD MEDALS

Chardonnay 1986 — Sunday Times Vintage Festival
UK

Chardonnay 1986 — New York International Wine
Show

Sauvignon Blanc 1985 — International Wine and Spirit
Competition UK

1988

Chardonnay 1987 — Champion Chardonnay, Royal
Easter Show

GOLD MEDALS

Chardonnay 1987 — Royal Easter Show

Gewürztraminer 1987 — Sunday Times Vintage
Festival UK

Fumé Blanc 1987 — Royal Easter Show

1989

Sauvignon Blanc 1989 — Trophy, Air New Zealand
Wine Awards

Sauvignon Blanc 1989 — Top Sauvignon Blanc,
Decanter Award

GOLD MEDALS

Chardonnay 1987 — Intervin, New York

Rhine Riesling 1989 — Air New Zealand Wine Awards

Sauvignon Blanc 1987 — Intervin, New York

Sauvignon Blanc 1989 — Air New Zealand Wine
Awards

1990

Sauvignon Blanc Oak Aged 1989 — Top 100, Best
in Class, Sydney International Small Winemakers
Competition

Sauvignon Blanc Oak Aged 1989 — Best Wine Award,
Sydney International Small Winemakers Competition

GOLD MEDALS

Chardonnay 1989 — Royal Easter Show

Sauvignon Blanc 1989 — *WINE* Magazine International
Challenge

Sauvignon Blanc Oak Aged 1989 — Royal Easter Show

Sauvignon Blanc Oak Aged 1989 — *WINE* Magazine
International Challenge

1991

Cabernet Sauvignon 1988 — Best in Class, Royal Easter
Show

GOLD MEDALS

Sauvignon Blanc 1991 — Air New Zealand Wine
Awards

Sauvignon Blanc Oak Aged 1989 — International Wine
and Spirit Competition UK

1992

Sauvignon Blanc 1991 — Wine of the Show, Sunday Times Vintage Festival UK

Sauvignon Blanc 1991 — Marquis de Goulaine Trophy, International Wine and Spirit Competition UK

Sauvignon Blanc 1991 — Highly Commended, *Decanter*

GOLD MEDALS

Chardonnay 1991 — Hobart Royal Agricultural Show

Chardonnay 1991 — Air New Zealand Wine Awards

Sauvignon Blanc 1991 — Sunday Times Vintage Festival UK

Sauvignon Blanc 1991 — International Wine and Spirit Competition UK

Sauvignon Blanc Oak Aged 1991 — ACI Australian Wine Show

Sauvignon Blanc Oak Aged 1991 — Air New Zealand Wine Awards

1993

GOLD MEDAL

Sauvignon Blanc Oak Aged 1992 — Expovina, Switzerland

JANE HUNTER

Awarded an OBE for her services to the New Zealand wine industry

HUNTER'S

Awarded the Tradenz Air New Zealand Export Excellence Award for a Regional Exporter

1994

GOLD MEDALS

Riesling 1993 — Sydney International Winemakers Top 100

Riesling 1994 — Canberra Wine Show

Riesling 1994 — National Wine Show Australia

Sauvignon Blanc 1993 — Royal Easter Show

Sauvignon Blanc 1994 — Hobart Royal Agricultural Show

Sauvignon Blanc Oak Aged 1993 — Royal Easter Show

Sauvignon Blanc Oak Aged 1993 — Intervin, New York

1995

Black Diamond Award, Intervin, New York, awarded to companies that win three gold medals

GOLD MEDALS

Chardonnay 1992 — Intervin, New York

Sauvignon Blanc Oak Aged 1993 — Intervin, New York

Sauvignon Blanc 1994 — Intervin, New York

Sauvignon Blanc 1994 — Liquorland Royal Easter Show

1996

Sauvignon Blanc Oak Aged 1994 — *Decanter* Award

GOLD MEDALS

Chardonnay 1994 — Sydney International Wine Competition

Chardonnay 1994 — Intervin, New York

Sauvignon Blanc 1995 — Sydney International Wine Competition

1997

Sauvignon Blanc 1997 — People's Choice Trophy, Christchurch Casino

GOLD MEDALS

Sauvignon Blanc 1996 — Sydney International Wine Competition

Chardonnay 1995 — WINPAC Wine Show Hong Kong

Riesling 1996 — Liquorland Top 100

Riesling 1997 — Perth Royal Wine Show

Sauvignon Blanc 1997 — Air New Zealand Wine Awards

Sauvignon Blanc/Chardonnay 1997 — Royal Agricultural Society of Tasmania

JANE HUNTER

Awarded an Honorary Doctorate in Science by Massey University

1998

MiruMiru™ 1995 — James Rogers Memorial Trophy, International Wine Challenge, UK

GOLD MEDALS

MiruMiru™ 1995 — International Wine Challenge, UK

Sauvignon Blanc 1998 — Air New Zealand Wine Awards

1999

GOLD MEDALS

Riesling 1998 — Sydney International Top 100

Sauvignon Blanc 1998 — Expovina, Switzerland

2000

GOLD MEDALS

Sauvignon Blanc 1999 — Sydney International Top 100

Sauvignon Blanc 1999 — Concours International Des Vins Switzerland

Sauvignon Blanc 2000 — Concours International Des Vins Switzerland

Sauvignon Blanc 2000 — Royal Hobart International Wine Show

2001

Sauvignon Blanc 2000 — Best White Wine of the Show, Sunday Times Wine Festival UK

GOLD MEDALS

Sauvignon Blanc 2000 — Sydney International Top 100

Sauvignon Blanc 2000 — Sunday Times Wine Festival UK

Sauvignon Blanc 2001 — National Off-Licence Association Irish Wine Show

Sauvignon Blanc 2001 — Royal Hobart International Wine Show

Hunter's Brut 1997 — Air New Zealand Wine Awards

Spring Creek Sauvignon Blanc/Chardonnay 2000 — Liquorland Top 100

2002

GOLD MEDALS

Sauvignon Blanc 2001 — Sydney International Top 100

Chardonnay 1999 — Blue-Gold, Sydney International
Top 100

Sauvignon Blanc 2001 — Intervin, USA

Pinot Noir 2000 — Intervin, USA

Sauvignon Blanc 2001 — Sunday Times Wine Club
Vintage Festival UK

MiruMiru™ 2000 — Air New Zealand Wine Awards

2003

GOLD MEDALS

Sauvignon Blanc 2002 — Sydney International Top 100

Chardonnay 2001 — Blue-Gold, Sydney International
Top 100

Riesling 2002 — Blue-Gold, Sydney International
Top 100

Riesling 2002 — Royal Hobart International Wine Show

Riesling 2002 — Hyatt National Riesling Challenge

Sauvignon Blanc 2002 — Sunday Times Wine Club
Vintage Festival UK

Riesling 2002 — Perth Royal Wine Show

Chardonnay 2001 — Perth Royal Wine Show

Sauvignon Blanc 2002 — Old Ebbitt Grill International
Wine for Oysters Competition

Riesling 2003 — Air New Zealand Wine Awards

MiruMiru™ 1999 — Effervescents du Monde, France

JANE HUNTER

Winner of the Inaugural International Women in Wine Award

2004

Rosé 2004 — Champion Rosé, Air New Zealand Wine Awards

Riesling 2004 — Champion Riesling, Royal Hobart International Wine Show

MiruMiru™ — Commended, *Decanter* World Wines

MiruMiru™ — 4 stars plus Top 5 status, *Cuisine* November 2004

Sauvignon Blanc 2004 — 4 stars, *Cuisine* December 2004

Pinot Noir 2002 — Highly Commended, Sydney International Wine Show

Pinot Noir 2003 — Highly Commended, Sydney International Wine Show

GOLD MEDALS

Sauvignon Blanc 2003 — Blue-Gold, Sydney International Top 100

Sauvignon Blanc 2003 — Perth Royal Wine Show

Sauvignon Blanc 2004 — Royal Hobart International Wine Show

Sauvignon Blanc 2004 — Vintage Cellars Wine Show of Australia, Canberra

Rosé 2004 — Air New Zealand Wine Awards

Riesling 2003 — Royal Easter Wine Show

Riesling 2004 — Vintage Cellars Wine Show of Australia, Canberra

Riesling 2004 — Royal Hobart International Wine Show

Chardonnay 2001 — Air New Zealand Wine Awards

Chardonnay 2002 — Perth Royal Wine Show

Chardonnay 2002 — Red Hill Show International 'Cool Climate Wine Show'

Gewürztraminer 2004 — Royal Hobart International Wine Show

Pinot Noir 2002 — Royal Hobart International Wine Show

2005

Pinot Noir 2002 — Best Pinot Noir, Red Hill Show International 'Cool Climate Wine Show'

Riesling 2004 — Bob Campbell's Best Value buy under $25, *New Zealand Home & Entertaining* June/July 2005

Pinot Noir 2004 — Best in Class, International Wine and Spirit Competition UK

Pinot Noir 2003 — 4 stars and Highly Commended, *Decanter* October 2005

Sauvignon Blanc 2005 — 5 stars, *Winestate* 'Best of recent releases' November/December 2005

Riesling 2004 — Best Wine, WINPAC Wine Show, Hong Kong

MiruMiru™ Reserve 2001 — 4½ stars, *Winestate* 'Best of recent releases' November/December 2005

Chardonnay 2004 — 4 stars, *Winestate* 'Best of recent releases' November/December 2005

GOLD MEDALS

Chardonnay 2002 — Royal Easter Wine Show

Pinot Noir 2002 — Red Hill Show International 'Cool Climate Wine Show'

MiruMiru™ 2002 — Liquorland Top 100

MiruMiru™ 2002 — Air New Zealand Wine Awards

Sauvignon Blanc 2004 — Old Ebbitt Grill International Wine for Oysters Competition

Riesling 2004 — Top Gold, WINPAC Wine Show, Hong Kong

Gewürztraminer 2005 — Air New Zealand Wine Awards

Hunter's Brut 2000 — WINPAC Wine Show, Hong Kong

2006

Pinot Noir 2005 — Top 100, Sydney International Wine Show

Pinot Noir 2004 — 4 stars, *Winestate* March/April 2006

Gewürztraminer 2005 — Highly Commended, Sydney International Wine Show

Gewürztraminer 2005 — 4 stars, *Winestate* March/ April 2006

Gewürztraminer 2005 — 4½ stars, *Cuisine* May 2006

Gewürztraminer 2006 — Trophy, Liquorland Top 100

Sauvignon Blanc 2005 — Highly Commended, Sydney International Wine Show

Sauvignon Blanc 2005 — 5 stars, *Winestate* March/April 2006

Riesling 2005 — 5 stars, *Winestate* March/April 2006

Riesling 2005 — 4 stars, *Cuisine* May 2006

Riesling 2006 — Top 10, Hyatt International Riesling Challenge, Australia

Chardonnay 2004 — 4½ stars, *Winestate* March/April 2006

Chardonnay 2003 — 4 stars, *Winestate* March/April 2006

Chardonnay 2003 — 4 stars, *Cuisine* September 2006

Kaho Roa 2003 — 4 stars, *Winestate* March/April 2006

Hukapapa 2004 — 4 stars, *Winestate* September/ October 2006

MiruMiru™ 2003 — Best in Class, International Wine and Spirit Competition, London

MiruMiru™ 2003 — 4 Stars, *Cuisine* July 2006

MiruMiru™ 2003 — 4 Stars, *Winestate* September/ October 2006

MiruMiru™ 2003 — Best Buy, *Cuisine* September 2006

Brookby Road 2004 — 4 stars, *Cuisine* September 2006

GOLD MEDALS

Pinot Noir 2004 — Blue-Gold, Sydney International Wine Show

Pinot Noir 2005 — Perth Royal Wine Show

Riesling 2005 — New World Wine Awards New Zealand

Riesling 2005 — Liquorland Top 100

Riesling 2006 — Hyatt International Riesling Challenge, Australia

Gewürztraminer 2006 — Liquorland Top 100

Kaho Roa 2004 — New Zealand International Wine Show

Chardonnay 2004 — Liquorland Top 100

Chardonnay 2004 — Air New Zealand Wine Awards

Chardonnay 2004 — Blue-Gold, Sydney International Wine Competition

2007

Chardonnay 2004 — 4 stars and Best Buy of the Tasting, *Cuisine* March 2007

Pinot Noir 2006 — Best of the Best, New World/Old World Single Varietal Red, American Express Tower Club Wine Awards

Sauvignon Blanc 2007 — Best Dry White Table Wine, Vintage Cellars National Wine Show of Australia

Sauvignon Blanc 2007 — Best Buy, *TiZwine*, November 2007

GOLD MEDALS

MiruMiru™ Reserve 2002 — Top Gold, WINPAC Wine Show, Hong Kong

Chardonnay 2004 — Royal Easter Show

Riesling 2006 — Vintage Cellars National Wine Show of Australia

Riesling 2007 — International Aromatic Wine Competition, Christchurch A & P Association

Pinot Noir 2006 — American Express Tower Club Wine Awards

2008

GOLD MEDALS

Sauvignon Blanc 2007 — Vintage Cellars National Wine Show of Australia

Sauvignon Blanc 2007 — Royal Hobart International Wine Show

Pinot Noir 2006 — International Cool Climate Wine Show, Australia